COOKING WITH
JAZZ

Nancy Bethea Keenan

NANSITE PUBLISHING • HATTIESBURG

Cover Photo/Design by
NANCY BETHEA KEENAN

ISBN 0-9717224-0-4

Library of Congress Control Number: 2002090025

NANSITE PUBLISHING
60 Cornerstone Rd.
Hattiesburg, MS 39402
www.nansite.com

Printed in the USA by
BOURNE BROTHERS PRINTING CO., INC.
Hattiesburg, MS

Nancy Keenan enjoyed a 30-year career in diversified business environments, including personnel administration/management in hospital, hotel, and engineering firms; and 17 years as a Real Estate Broker, Appraiser and Certified Instructor (Louisiana).

She attended the following schools:
University of Mississippi (Ole Miss), Business Administration;
Delgado College, New Orleans, Real Estate Agent and Broker courses;
Appraisal Institute and National Association of Master Appraisers,
Real Estate Appraisal courses.

Nancy has always enjoyed cooking, entertaining and gardening.

"Cooking with Jazz" started with a collection of recipes from friends, family, New Orleans Times Picayune, New Orleans Public Service and many recipes developed by Nancy over the years.

Notes

DEDICATION

TO MY CHILDREN:

SON, David Keenan, who learned to cook at a very young age, and has become a really good cook. He was also, as a teenager, my all-time best gardener. David is super efficient in all endeavors. He calls to ask, "Mom, tell me exactly how you make the Coon Balls".

GRANDSON, Jasper "Jazz" Keenan, who learned to love the kitchen at age two, when we were dyeing Easter eggs. Jazz is a wonderful helper in the kitchen and especially loves preparing for a dinner party. He says, "Nan, when are you having friends over for dinner? Don't do it without me". He also calls to ask, "Nan, tell me one more time how you make the tuna salad".

TO MY PARENTS:

MOM, Margaret May Bethea, who gave me my first cooking lessons, including all the lagniappe she had always provided: homemade pickles, relishes, jams, jellies, Christmas fruit cakes and candies (fudge, divinity and date nut loaf). And David says, "Oh, don't forget MaMa's butter cakes".

AND TO THE MEMORY OF MY DAD, Jasper David Bethea, who would have loved to be in on this project—especially the cooking and tasting. He was a positive influence on all who knew him, and always exhibited his keen wit and sense of humor.

ACKNOWLEDGMENT

My sincere appreciation to Richard Norman for his dedication in this project, and acting as my computer consultant, chief editor, and master of tenacity.

Thanks to my Mom for being my chief consultant in ingredients, vessel size, cooking time/temperatures and yields; all things worthwhile... and a few others too!

What fond memories of my aunt Winnie Bethea Catt, who was a great cook and piqued my interest in cooking; and who shared many of her wonderful recipes.

Thanks to my aunt Ella May Loper, who, with her daughter Patricia Maggio, did all of the Holiday cooking for our family for so many years. She could put on the biggest spread of wonderful food, with the greatest of ease. What a superb cook!

Thanks also to all my taste-testing friends, and to those who have so generously shared their wonderful food and recipes.

INTRODUCTION

My collection of recipes comes from friends and co-workers in New Orleans (for plus 25 years); and bridge club friends in Houston, who were predominately retired teachers and professional business women. Kudos to working women everywhere, most of whom rank among the world's best cooks! Many of the ole-time New Orleans restaurants recipes came from New Orleans Public Service and the Times Picayune. Also included are many of my own original recipes.

I started cooking at age 10--fried chicken, rice and milk gravy. I poured the gravy out eight times, and on the ninth time, Daddy assured me that "The gravy is just fine--it is real good". This was also my first lesson in recognizing a not so "little" white lie!

My desire for homecooked food became overwhelming while living in a dormitory and eating three meals a day in a school cafeteria, FOR THREE YEARS!

As a young working Mother and trying to spend as much time at home as possible, I developed a love for gardening and cooking. We cooked a lot on weekends, and frequently invited friends over for lunch or dinner.

What a surprise to find tucked back in Mom's recipe files were many of the same recipes I have collected through the years. Mom's recipe files date back to 1937, and include a few of my Grandmother's--some in her handwriting. Many of the ole-time recipes have been revised to reduce the amount of salt, sugar and "lard".

My Bethea grandparents, "Fama and Bob", worked together as a team in the kitchen. Bob was in charge of the cornbread and when it was just the two of them, or the three of us, he made small hoecakes.

My Bethea grandparents owned a country grocery and lumber company. When Bob was in the woods with the logging crew, Fama ran the store and would "scale" the lumber for a buyer (in her feminine attire).

The grocery carried canned goods, flour, and basic baking ingredients. The large flour bags were made of printed cotton fabric, suitable for making clothes, albeit a poor quality of fabric. In the winter months they sold hoop cheese. The drink machine was cooled by circulating water. The two big sellers were Moon Pies and RC Colas. This was pure economics – the Moon Pie and RC Cola were about the largest snack and drink you could get for a nickle each. In later years there was a small freezer for ice cream products.

The store also sold Gulf gasoline and kerosene. The orange kerosene tank (with a pump on top) was about the size of a 2000 model 4-burner electric or gas stove.

The store was also a designated voting site and election days were as exciting as the State Fair ... well almost! I was enthralled with the vote counting; and loved "working" in the store.

TO DISPEL A MYTH--about Grits and Southerners: I was raised in the South; my parents and grandparents were all Mississippians; yet, my earliest recollection of eating grits was when I was in high school--in the restaurant in the old Heidelberg Hotel in Jackson. I do not remember either of my grandmothers ever cooking grits. My Grandmother "Fama" May cooked rice for breakfast, which she probably learned from living in a logging camp in Louisiana as a young bride.

Whatever you cook, whenever you cook, please remember to share with an older person living alone. If it is someone you will not see within the next day or two, freeze a container of food for them, and make an effort to get it to them. The very best thing you can do for an older person is to TAKE THEM SOME HOME COOKED FOOD!

BON JOUR   BON SOIR   BON APPÉTIT

Table of Contents

Notes

APPETIZERS

AVOCADO MOUSSE

½ c. mayonnaise
1 c. hot water
5-6 sprigs parsley
½ tsp. salt
¾ c. whipping cream

1 (3 oz.) pkg. lime Jell-O
Juice of 1 small lemon
2 c. ripe avocado, mashed
  (about 2½ average size)
¼ c. finely grated onion

Dissolve Jell-O in water; cool in refrigerator until syrupy; peel and puree avocado; combine onion, salt, mayonnaise, lemon juice, and finely chopped parsley; add to avocado. Beat cream stiff, stir into mixture gently; add syrupy Jell-O; mix carefully then pour into medium ring mold and chill until solid.

Unmold when ready to serve. Fill center with cut up chicken or seafood that has been mixed with a little French Dressing. Yield: Serves 20 as a spread.

PARTY BROCCOLI

½ tsp. black pepper
1 Tbsp. soy sauce
2 Tbsp. chives
Parmesan cheese
Dash Tabasco

1 (8 oz.) pkg. cream cheese
2 pkg. frozen broccoli spears
1 can cream of shrimp soup
¾ c. toasted almonds

Cook broccoli and drain well. Blend soup and cream cheese over low heat; add soy sauce, Tabasco, black pepper and chives; pour over broccoli; sprinkle with Parmesan cheese; garnish with toasted almonds. Yield: Serves 20 as a spread.

TOMATO ASPIC

2 Tbsp. lemon juice	1 envelope unflavored gelatin
¼ tsp. salt	1¾ c. tomato juice, divided
½ tsp. sugar	½ tsp. Worcestershire
⅛ tsp. Tabasco	

Sprinkle gelatin on ½ cup tomato juice to soften; place over low heat and stir until gelatin dissolves; remove from heat, and stir in remaining tomato juice and seasonings; turn into a two cup mold or individual molds; chill until firm; unmold on serving plate; garnish with salad greens, cucumber slices and ripe olives; serve with salad dressing. Yield: 4 servings.

MOCK OYSTER DIP

8 Tbsp. butter	1 pkg. chopped frozen broccoli
1 large onion, minced	1 can cream of mushroom soup
1 can mushrooms	1 (6 oz.) roll garlic cheese
Dash Tabasco	

Cook broccoli until overdone; sauté onions in butter; add cream of mushroom soup, mushrooms and juice; break up garlic cheese and add to mixture; add Tabasco and broccoli; keep warm in chafing dish; eat with potato chips. Can also be used in patty shells, or over noodles as a casserole. Yield: Serves 15 as a spread.

SHRIMP DIP

1 c. ground shrimp
1 c. mayonnaise
1 tsp. dry mustard
2 Tbsp. catsup
Dash Tabasco

1 (8 oz.) pkg. cream cheese
1 medium onion, finely diced
1 tsp. Worcestershire sauce
Pinch salt & pepper

Mix together well. Yield: Serves 12-15 as spread.

SHRIMP MOLD

1½ lbs. shrimp, boiled
2 Tbsp. water
1 Tbsp. lemon juice
¾ c. mayonnaise
Tabasco to taste

1 can golden mushroom soup
1 envelope unflavored gelatin
1 (8 oz.) pkg. cream cheese
1 bunch shallots, minced
1 c. finely chopped celery

Soften gelatin in 2 Tbsp. water. Lightly grease mold with mayonnaise; heat soup; mix in softened cream cheese until melted; remove from heat; stir in softened gelatin; add remaining ingredients and blend thoroughly. Turn into greased mold and chill until firm. Unmold. Yield: Serves 20 as spread.

*Can substitute crab meat, then use regular cream of mushroom soup.

GARLIC CHEESE BALLS

16 oz. cream cheese
1 tsp. garlic, minced
½ tsp. cayenne pepper

8 oz. sharp cheddar cheese
8 oz. extra sharp cheddar cheese

Grate cheese and allow to soften at room temperature. Mix all ingredients together and blend in mixer; shape into balls and sprinkle with paprika or parsley. Serve with crackers or party rye. Yield: Serves 30 as spread.

SWEET & SOUR SAUSAGE BALLS

2 lb. pork sausage	1½ c. catsup
2 eggs, beaten	6 Tbsp. brown sugar
¾ c. soft bread crumbs	¼ c. wine vinegar
¼ c. soy sauce	Salad oil

Combine sausage, eggs, bread crumbs and shape into teaspoon size balls; sauté in oil until brown; drain. Combine the remaining ingredients, pour over the balls and simmer 30 minutes. Balls may be refrigerated or frozen in sauce. To serve, heat at 350°F for 20 minutes. Yield: 5½ dozen.

COON BALLS
(David's Favorite)

3½ c. Bisquick	8 oz. extra sharp cheddar cheese
1 lb. hot sausage	Cayenne pepper to taste

Grate cheese, and allow cheese and sausage to come to room temperature, or slightly warm sausage in microwave and mix with grated cheese; knead Bisquick into sausage and cheese; shape into ½ inch balls; flatten into small biscuits for more uniform cooking; bake at 330°F approximately 20 minutes or until golden brown; turn after 10 minutes. Yield: 9 dozen. Great for breakfast.

Hint: Freeze and bag; thaw in microwave before baking.

HORSERADISH & BACON DIP

1 env. onion soup mix	2 c. sour cream
3 Tbsp. horseradish	6 slices crisp bacon, crumbled

Blend all ingredients and refrigerate 8 hours.
Yield: Approximately 2 cups.

CUCUMBER RING

1 Tbsp. lemon juice
3 Tbsp. lemon juice
1 c. boiling water
¾ c. cold water
2 Tbsp. sugar
¾ tsp. salt
Lettuce
Cherry tomatoes (optional)

1 pkg. unflavored gelatin
1 (3 oz.) pkg. lemon gelatin
1 (8 oz.) pkg. cream cheese
1 cucumber, thinly sliced
4 cucumbers, shredded
1 c. mayonnaise
½ c. snipped parsley

Dissolve lemon-flavored gelatin in boiling water, add the cold water
and 1 Tbsp. lemon juice; pour into a deep 6½ inch mold; chill until
partially set (consistency of egg white); overlap the thinly sliced
cucumber atop gelatin mixture in mold; press into gelatin; chill until
almost firm. Meanwhile, in saucepan mix the sugar, salt and
unflavored gelatin until dissolved; stir in 3 Tbsp. lemon juice. With
rotary beater, gradually beat hot gelatin mixture into softened cream
cheese until smooth. Peel and halve 4 cucumbers lengthwise, scrape
out seeds, finely shred or grind, drain (approximately 1½ c.); stir
ground cucumber, mayonnaise, parsley and onion into cream cheese
mixture. Pour over almost firm gelatin mold. Chill until firm. Unmold
onto lettuce lined plate; garnish with cherry tomatoes.
Yield: Serves 12-15 as an appetizer.

CHILE CON QUESO

2 lb. Velveeta cheese,
    chunked
1 c. salsa

¼ lb. sharp cheddar cheese, grated
6-7 (or 2 cans) green chile
    peppers, chopped

Combine and melt. Serve hot or cold. Yield: 4 cups.

SPINACH DIP

1 c. sour cream	1 (10 oz.) pkg. frozen spinach
1 c. mayonnaise	(uncooked) thawed & drained
1 Tbsp. onion, minced	1 pkg. vegetable soup mix
2 Tbsp. Parmesan cheese	1 (8 oz.) can water chestnuts, chopped
½ tsp. Creole seasoning	

Combine all ingredients and refrigerate overnight.
Yield: Serves 15 to 20 as a spread.

Serve with chips, piquante, guacamole and sour cream.

PARTY BEEF BALLS

1 egg, beaten	2 lbs. lean ground beef
1 tsp. soy sauce	2 medium onions, minced
½ tsp. black pepper	1 Tbsp. Worcestershire sauce
2 tsp. salt	½ tsp. red pepper (optional)
1 tsp. oregano	¼ c. salad oil
1½ c. barbeque sauce	

Mix all ingredients (except oil and barbeque sauce) together and
shape into 50 to 60 very small balls. In a heavy skillet, heat oil & cook
meatballs until done. In microwave, heat barbeque sauce until warm.
Transfer meatballs to chafing dish over low heat; cover with warm
barbeque sauce; use toothpicks for serving. Yield: 50 to 60.

PICKLED SHRIMP

2-2½ lbs. shrimp
(fresh or frozen)
7-8 bay leaves
1½ c. diced celery

2 c. sliced onions
¼ c. mixed pickling spices
Crab boil
Salt to taste

Cover shrimp with boiling water; add celery, spices, salt and crab boil; cover and simmer 5 minutes; drain and de-vein under cold water; alternate shrimp, onions and bay leaves in shallow baking dish.

Pickling Marinade:
1½ c. salad oil
3 Tbs. capers & juice
¾ c. white vinegar

2½ tsp. celery seed
Dash Tabasco sauce
1½ tsp. salt

Combine, mix well; pour over cooked shrimp; cover; chill at least 24 hours, spooning marinade over shrimp. These shrimp will keep in refrigerator for at least a week. Remove bay leaves before serving. Yield: Serves about 6.

TEX-MEX DIP

1 c. bean dip
2 tsp. lemon juice
1 c. sour cream
½ c. mayonnaise
8 oz. shredded cheddar
  cheese

2 avocados mashed
  (or guacamole)
1 pkg. taco seasoning mix
1 sm. can chopped ripe olives
1 bunch shallots, chopped
1 large tomato, chopped

1st layer - Spread bean dip out on a shallow dish
2nd layer - Avocado (or guacamole) mixed with lemon juice
3rd layer - Mixture of sour cream, mayonnaise and taco seasoning
4th layer - Shallots
5th layer - Ripe olives and tomatoes

Cover with shredded cheddar cheese; serve with chips.
Yield: Serves 6-8 as appetizer.

SWEET & PUNGENT FRANKS

2 Tbsp. vegetable oil	2 pkg. (5½ oz.) little weiners
2 Tbsp. cornstarch	2 (15¼ oz.) cans pineapple chunks in
1 tsp. sugar	heavy syrup
½ tsp. salt	1 large green pepper, cut in 1 inch
¼ c. cider vinegar	squares

Drain pineapple; reserve syrup; heat oil in large skillet over medium heat; add green peppers; saute' 2 minutes, stirring occasionally; remove; reserve. Add wieners to skillet; cook until lightly browned; blend reserved syrup, vinegar, cornstarch, sugar and salt in bowl; pour into skillet; bring to boil, stirring constantly; add pineapple & green peppers; heat through. Serve with toothpicks.
Yield: Serves 12-15 as appetizer.

GUACAMOLE DIP

2 ripe avocados	⅓ tsp. red pepper
1 tsp. salt	3 dashes Tabasco (optional)
2 Tbsp. grated onion	1 tsp. Worcestershire sauce
1½ tsp. lemon juice	1 clove garlic, minced

Peel and mash avocados. Add salt and lemon juice. Stir in Worcestershire sauce, Tabasco, garlic, pepper, and onion. Serve with chips. Yield: 1½ cups.

SALAMI STACKS

¼ c. sour cream
⅛ tsp. pepper
½ tsp. salt
½ c. prepared horseradish

2 (8 oz.) pkg. cream cheese, softened
56 slices hard salami
(approximately 1¼ lb. 3 inch salami,
cut ⅛ inch thick)

Combine cream cheese, horseradish, salt, pepper & sour cream, blend thoroughly. Reserve 8 slices salami (to top 8 stacks of 6 slices ea.); spread remainder with cream cheese mixture, allowing 1 Tbsp. for each slice; repeat with remainder. Cover with plastic wrap; chill several hours; cut stacks into eights; arrange on platter; chill until serving time. Yield: 64 pieces.

OLIVE CHEESE BALLS

2 Tbsp. soft butter
½ tsp. celery seed
Dash cayenne

1 c. shredded sharp cheddar cheese
2 (3 oz.) bottles stuffed olives
½ c. sifted all-purpose flour

Mix butter and cheese until smooth; blend in flour, cayenne and celery seeds; shape 1 tsp. dough around each olive to form a ball. Place on baking sheet; bake at 400°F for 15 minutes. Serve hot or cold.

To freeze, place uncooked balls about ½ inch apart on baking sheet (make sure balls do not touch); cover with foil and put in freezer. After cheese balls are thoroughly frozen, remove from baking sheet and store in freezer bags. To serve, place frozen cheese balls on baking sheet; bake at 400°F for 18 to 20 minutes. Yield: about 3 dozen.

SALMON BALLS

1 large can red salmon, drained and flaked
3 tsp. horseradish
¼ Tbsp. liquid smoke
Parsley flakes

1 (8 oz.) pkg. softened cream cheese
1 Tbsp. lemon juice
3 tsp. grated onion
¼ tsp. salt

Combine all ingredients and shape into balls; roll balls in parsley flakes. Yield: approximately 20 balls.

TEXAS CAVIAR

1 large jar piquant sauce (medium or hot)
1 Tbsp. sugar
1 tsp. salt
2 Tbsp. ground cumin
1-16 oz. can white hominy, drained
¼ c. seeded & chopped jalapeño peppers

1 c. diced green pepper
1 c. chopped white onion
1 c. chopped fresh tomato
2 Tbsp. coarsely ground black pepper
½ c. finely chopped cilantro
2 (16 oz.) cans black eyed peas, drained
1 c. chopped green onions (include green tops)

Mix all the ingredients well. Marinate in the refrigerator for 24 hours. Serve with triangular corn tortilla chips. Yield: approximately 6 cups.

CALIFORNIA VEGETABLE DIP

1 env. onion soup mix
2 c. sour cream
2 tsp. chili powder

1 c. finely chopped green pepper
1 c. finely chopped tomato

Combine all ingredients; serve as dip. Yield: 2 cups.

CRAB MEAT SANDWICHES

2 Tbsp. chili sauce
1 chopped onion
2 Tbsp. mayonnaise

1 can crab meat, drained
1 can shrimp, drained
1 (8 oz.) pkg. cream cheese
Dash Worcestershire sauce

Put all ingredients in mixer and blend well; spread on bread; cut into finger sandwiches. Yield: Approximately 24 finger sandwiches.

DILL DIP

1 c. mayonnaise
1 c. sour cream
2 tsp. dill weed
½ tsp. celery seed

1½ tsp. dill pickle juice
1½ tsp. parsley flakes
1½ Tbsp. onion flakes
1½ tsp. Accent or Creole seasoning

Combine all ingredients; refrigerate for 8 hours; serve as a spread. Yield: Approximately 2 cups.

CAPONATO

1 eggplant, diced (un-peeled)
½ c. chopped celery
2 Tbsp. sugar
2½ Tbsp. white wine vinegar
14 oz. pasta sauce
½ tsp. Creole seasoning
Salt to taste

¼ c. olive oil
¾ c. pitted ripe olives, sliced
½ c. salad olives, chopped
1 medium onion, chopped
1 medium green bell pepper, chopped
1 (3½ oz.) jar capers, drained

In large skillet, sauté eggplant, onion ,green pepper and celery in oil. Add pasta sauce, ripe olives, salad olives, sugar, vinegar and capers; cover, reduce heat and simmer 30 minutes, stirring frequently. Stir in salt and Creole seasoning; remove from heat and cool. Chill 24 hours; serve with crackers. Yield: 1-2 cups.

BLUE CHEESE WREATH

1 Tbsp. milk	2 (8 oz.) pkg. cream cheese, softened
1/8 tsp. salt	1 lb. blue cheese, crumbled
1/4 tsp. white pepper	3/4 c. green pepper, chopped
1 whole pimento	1 (4 oz.) jar pimentos, drained & finely
1/4 c. dried parsley flakes	chopped
Crackers or party rye bread	1 med. onion, finely chopped

In large mixer bowl combine cream cheese, blue cheese, and milk; beat until smooth; add green pepper, onion, chopped pimento, salt, and pepper; mix until combined. On large serving platter, shape cheese mixture into a ring the shape of a wreath. Sprinkle top and sides with parsley. Use whole pimento to make ribbon for the garnish. Chill. Serve with crackers or party rye bread. Yield: Serves 20 as a spread.

HAM SANDWICH SPREAD

1 small onion, minced	1 c. butter softened
1 Tbsp. poppy seed	1 tsp. Worcestershire sauce
2 tsp. Dijon mustard	Swiss cheese
Ham	Rye bread

Mix and serve. Yield: 1½ cup.

DEVILED EGGS

6 hard boiled eggs	1 (3 oz.) can deviled ham
1 Tbsp. minced onion	6 Tbsp. mayonnaise
½ tsp. dry mustard	1/4 c. sweet relish
½ tsp. celery seed	Creole seasoning to taste

Peel and cut eggs in half. Mash egg yolks with fork and add other ingredients. Mix well and stuff eggs. Yield: 12 servings.

JEZEBEL CRANBERRIES

½ c. water
1 Tbsp. Dijon mustard
3 Tbsp. prepared horseradish

1 (12 oz.) bag cranberries, fresh or
  frozen
½ c. granulated sugar
½ c. firmly packed brown sugar

Combine water, granulated sugar and brown sugar in a medium saucepan; stir well. Bring to a boil over medium heat; add the cranberries; return to a boil, and cook 10 minutes, stirring occasionally. Spoon into a bowl; let cool to room temperature. Stir in horseradish and mustard. Serve chilled. Store in an airtight container for up to 1 week. Pour over cream cheese and serve with crackers or party rye. Yield: 2½ cups (serving size; ¼ cup).

Also may be served with beef or pork.

GALATOIRE'S SHRIMP REMOULADE

⅔ c. olive oil
5 Tbsp. Creole mustard
2 Tbsp. paprika
⅓ c. vinegar
2 cloves garlic
Dash Tabasco sauce

1 lb. shrimp, boiled, peeled
  and de-veined
1 Tbsp. prepared horseradish
1 bunch green onion
1 stalk celery
1 bunch parsley
Salt & black pepper to taste

In a food processor chop all vegetables very fine; remove to a ceramic or glass bowl; add mustard, paprika, horseradish, Tabasco and salt and black pepper to taste. Add vinegar and gradually add olive oil while whisking; fold in shrimp and let marinate several hours or overnight in refrigerator. Serve cold over shredded lettuce. Yield: 4 servings.

GALATOIRE'S OYSTERS en BROCHETTE

2 doz. raw oysters	12 strips bacon, cut in half
4 (8 in.) skewers	1 egg
¾ c. milk	Salt and pepper to taste
Flour	Oil for deep fat frying

Fry bacon until not quite crisp; alternate six oysters and six half strips of bacon (folded) on each skewer; make a batter with egg and milk and season well with salt and pepper; dip each skewer in batter, roll in flour and deep fry until golden brown. Serve on toast points with lemon wedges. Yield: 6 skewers.

BOILED PEANUTS

Select young green peanuts. Clean, wash and put in cooker; cover with boiling water with 1 Tbsp. of salt per quart of water; continue to add water and salt and boil for approximately 2 hours (or until peanuts inside the shell are tender). Cool and serve (on the Patio!!!).

For HOT boiled peanuts use Zatarain's Liquid Crab Boil.

POPCORN

Pop unsalted corn in air popper in microwave; pour corn in clean paper bag, add Gardetto's snack mix or salted peanuts and shake bag Serve.

BEVERAGES

WINE

4 c. sugar   1 large can grape juice
1 pkg. yeast   1 small can grape juice

Place in 1 gallon jar and stir well. Let set 21 to 31 days.

CAFÉ AU LAIT

Pour into serving cup ½ cup boiling milk and ½ cup hot, strong coffee. Serve with beignets.

Popular in New Orleans (French Quarter sidewalk cafes).

SPICED TEA MIX

2½ c. sugar   6 oz. dry lemonade crystals
2 c. Tang   1 tsp. ground cinnamon
1 tsp. ground cloves   ⅔ c. Lipton instant tea

Blend all ingredients and store in dry sealed jar. Add 3 heaping teaspoons to 1 cup boiling water per serving.

GINGER ALMOND TEA

1 c. boiling water
1¼ c. sugar
4 c. water
1 tsp. vanilla
1 tsp. almond extract

5 regular tea bags
(decaffeinated optional)
¾ c. lemon juice (bottled)
1 qt. ginger ale, chilled

Pour 1 cup boiling water over tea bags, cover and steep for 5 minutes. Remove tea bags; stir in sugar, water, lemon juice, vanilla extract and almond extract; stir; place in refrigerator; chill throughly. Just before serving add ginger ale and pour over ice. Yield: 10-12 servings.

MOCHA MIX

2 c. coffee creamer
2 c. powdered milk
2 c. sugar

1 c. cocoa
¼ c. instant coffee

Blend all ingredients. Store in airtight jar. To use, place 2 rounded teaspoonfuls in a cup of boiling water.

MOCK CHAMPAGNE

4 c. sugar
4 c. water

2 c. orange juice
4 c. grape or pineapple juice
8 pt. chilled ginger ale

Boil sugar and water for 3 minutes and cool. Add rest of juices and chill. Just before serving add chilled ginger ale. Yield: 50 servings.

PARTY PUNCH

1 c. powdered sugar
¼ c. fresh lemon juice

1 (46 oz.) can pineapple juice
1 (6 oz.) can frozen orange juice
1 large bottle chilled ginger ale

Have all juices chilled. Combine pineapple and orange juices; melt powdered sugar in lemon juice; add to mixture. Add ginger ale just before serving. Yield: 2½ quarts.

COCOA MIX

2 c. powdered milk
1 c. cocoa

1 c. powdered sugar
⅓ c. powdered non-dairy creamer
(optional)

Blend all ingredients. Store in airtight jar. To use, place 4 rounded teaspoonfuls into a large cup and fill with boiling water. Whipped cream or marshmallows may be added as an enhancement.

SANGRIAS

Blackberry wine
Grapefruit juice

Oranges
Cherries

Mix blackberry wine and grapefruit juice half and half, or to taste; garnish with orange slice and a cherry.

SHERRY COOLER

2 c. dry sherry
½ c. brandy
Ice (optional)
Orange slices (optional)

1 c. orange liqueur
Lemon-lime carbonated beverage,
    chilled
Maraschino cherries (optional)

In a decanter combine dry sherry, orange liqueur and brandy. Chill throughly. Divide sherry mixture among 8 cocktail glasses. Add ice if desired. Fill each glass with about ½ cup chilled lemon-lime carbonated beverage. Stir. Garnish with orange slices and cherries, if desired. Yield: 8 servings.

BREADS & MUFFINS

ORANGE DATE MUFFINS

1 c. buttermilk
2 large eggs
1 c. butter, softened
1 Tbsp. butter, melted
1 tsp. vanilla extract
1 c. chopped pecans
1 c. chopped dates

2 tsp. baking soda
3 c. all-purpose flour
2 c. light brown sugar, firmly packed
¼ c. grated orange rind
⅓ c. powdered sugar
2 Tbsp. fresh orange juice

Stir together buttermilk and soda until blended; beat 1 c. butter at medium speed with an electric mixer until creamy; gradually add brown sugar, beating well. Stir in buttermilk mixture, eggs, flour, orange rind, vanilla until blended; fold in pecans and dates. Spoon batter into greased muffin pans, filling ⅔ full. Bake at 350°F for 20-23 minutes; cool on wire rack. Stir together powdered sugar, orange juice and melted butter; drizzle glaze evenly over muffins. Yield: 1½ dozen.

Note: Batter may be covered tightly and stored in refrigerator up to 24 hours.

HAZELNUT PANCAKES

2 c. Bisquick
1 egg
1 c. milk
8 oz. whipped cream

2 Tbsp. packed brown sugar
2 Tbsp. hazelnut cream
1 tsp. almond extract
3 c. berries, sliced peaches, apples or Bananas Supreme

Beat all ingredients except whipped cream and fruit with wire whisk or hand beater until well blended; pour by scant ¼ cupfuls onto hot griddle (grease griddle if necessary). Cook until pancakes are dry around the edges; turn; cook until golden brown. Top with fruit and whipped cream. Yield: 12 pancakes.

ANGEL BISCUITS

1 pkg. dry yeast	1 tsp. baking powder
¼ c. warm water	1 tsp. salt
2½ c. flour	2 Tbsp. sugar
½ tsp. baking soda	½ c. shortening
1 c. buttermilk	

Dissolve the yeast in warm water, set aside. Mix dry ingredients, flour, baking soda, baking powder, salt and sugar, cut in the shortening; stir in the buttermilk and yeast mixture; blend thoroughly; dough is ready to refrigerate or roll out into biscuits.

Turn the dough out onto a floured board and knead lightly; roll out and cut with a biscuit cutter, placing them in a greased pan. Let the dough rise slightly before baking in a 400°F. oven for about 12 to 15 minutes until lightly browned and done. If the dough is cold, you will need to let it set a little longer to rise. Yield: 1 dozen.

Note: Dough will keep up to three days in the refrigerator in a covered bowl.

BANANA-NUT MUFFINS

¼ c. sugar	2 c. all-purpose flour
1 c. milk	1 tsp. baking powder
1 egg, beaten	⅓ c. vegetable oil
1 c. water	1 c. mashed bananas
¾ c. chopped nuts	

Preheat oven to 400°F; grease a 12-cup muffin pan. Sift flour, sugar and baking powder into a medium bowl and make a well in center; mix milk, egg, water, oil, banana into well. Mix batter just until moistened; do not over mix; fold in pecans; spoon batter into prepared muffin cups; bake until a toothpick inserted into center comes out clean or until golden brown, about 15 minutes. Yield: 12 muffins.

BEIGNETS

1 c. milk	2 Tbsp. lukewarm water
1 egg	1 pkg. active dry or cake yeast
¼ c. sugar	2 Tbsp. vegetable oil
¾ tsp. salt	3½ c. sifted all-purpose flour
½ tsp. nutmeg	Sifted confectioners sugar

Scald milk. Add granulated sugar, salt, and nutmeg. Cool to lukewarm. Sprinkle or crumble yeast into warm water (use lukewarm water for cake yeast), stirring until yeast is dissolved.

To lukewarm milk mixture add oil, egg and dissolved yeast, blending with spoon. Add flour gradually, beating well. Cover with wax paper and let rise in warm place (about 85°F) until double in size.

Turn dough (it will be soft) onto well floured surface; knead gently. Roll into 18"x12" rectangle; cut into thirty-six 3"x2" rectangles. Cover with clean towel and let rise ½ hour.

Fry a few beignets at a time in deep fat (375°F) until golden brown. Drain on crumpled paper towels. Drop beignets in brown paper bag, sprinkle with confectioners sugar, and shake well until throughly coated. Serve piping hot with café au lait. Yield: 3 dozen.

MOCK BEIGNETS

2 cans refrigerated biscuits, plain
Hot grease
Sifted powdered sugar

Cut biscuits in half and roll flat with rolling pin; drop into hot frying grease, a few at a time; turn once. Watch carefully as they brown quickly. Drain on absorbent paper. Sprinkle with powdered sugar. Yield: 40 beignets.

DATE NUT MUFFINS

2 c. whole wheat flour	¾ c. chopped dates
1½ c. wheat germ	¾ c. chopped pecans
1½ c. bran	1 c. molasses
4 tsp. baking powder	4 Tbsp. honey
2 tsp. baking soda	2 eggs, beaten
½ c. raisins	4 Tbsp. cooking oil
1 c. buttermilk	Amaretto

Soak raisins in Ameretto to plump and zap in microwave for 30 seconds. Mix together flour, wheat germ, bran, baking soda & baking powder; mix in dates & pecans; blend together molasses, honey, oil, beaten eggs, raisins and buttermilk, add to dry ingredients and mix well; bake in muffin tins in 400°F oven for 15-20 minutes. Yield: 2 dozen.

BLUEBERRY MUFFINS

1 egg	2 c. Bisquick baking mix
⅓ c. sugar	¾ c. blueberries, fresh or frozen
⅔ c. milk	(thawed & drained)
2 Tbsp. vegetable oil	

Preheat oven to 400°F. Grease bottoms only of 12 medium muffin cups, 2x1¼ inch, or line with paper baking cups. Beat egg slightly in medium bowl; stir in remaining ingredients except blueberries just until moistened. Fold blueberries into batter; divide batter evenly among cups. Bake 15-18 minutes or until golden brown. Yield: 12 muffins.

BEER BISCUITS

3 c. Bisquick	2 Tbsp. sugar
12 oz. beer	

Mix thoroughly; roll and cut. Bake at 350°F for 10 minutes. Yield: 1½ dozen.

HUSH PUPPIES

1 c. corn meal	1 Tbsp. sugar (optional)
½ c. flour	2 tsp. baking powder
¼ tsp. salt	1 egg
¾ c. milk	1 medium onion, coarsely chopped

Mix dry ingredients with milk (mixture will be thick). Add onion and egg; beat. Refrigerate batter all day. Drop batter from a small spoon into deep fat; cook over medium heat for 3-5 minutes or until golden brown. Yield: 3 dozen.

SWEET POTATO BREAD

2 c. sifted flour	2 eggs beaten
¾ c. sugar	1 c. mashed sweet potato
1 tsp. baking powder	½ c. milk
¼ tsp. mace	3 Tbsp. melted shortening
½ c. chopped pecans	6 pecan halves

Sift together flour, sugar, baking powder, and mace; stir in chopped pecans and set aside. Blend together eggs, sweet potatoes, milk, shortening; add liquid to flour mixture, stirring until blended; turn into greased 4½x8½ inch loaf pan. Press pecan halves over top to form design. Bake at 350°F for 1 hour and 10 minutes. Cool in pan 10 minutes before removing from pan. Cool throughly before thinly slicing. Yield: Approximately 1 dozen slices.

EASY BUTTERMILK BISCUITS

1 c. buttermilk	1 stick butter, melted
	2½ c. self-rising flour

Mix flour with butter and buttermilk. Knead and roll biscuits on lightly floured board or pastry cloth; cut and bake at 400°F for 12 minutes or until lightly browned on top. Yield: 10-12 medium biscuits.

CAJUN HOT TOMATO BREAD

1 c. water	1 c. Bloody Mary mix
1/3 c honey	1 pkg. active dry yeast
1/4 c. vegetable oil	1/4 c. chopped green onion tops
1/4 c. chopped parsley	1 clove garlic, pressed
1 tsp. salt	5-6 c. all-purpose flour

Combine Bloody Mary mix in small saucepan; cook over low heat until mixture reaches 105°F to 115°F; pour into large warm bowl. Add yeast; stir until dissolved; add honey, oil, onion tops, parsley, garlic and salt; mix well. Add 1 cup flour and stir until smooth; stir in more flour until firm dough is formed. Knead dough on lightly floured board about 5 minutes or until smooth and elastic. Shape dough into a ball. Place in greased large bowl; turn to grease all sides. Cover bowl and set in warm place to rise about 1 hour until doubled in bulk.

Punch dough down and divide into two equal pieces. Roll each piece on lightly floured surface into rectangle. Roll each piece tightly from short side, jelly-roll style. Pinch seam to seal; place in greased 9x5x3-inch loaf pan. Cover and set in warm place to rise about 1 hour or until doubled in bulk.

Bake in preheated 400°F oven about 30 minutes or until loaves sound hollow when tapped and crust is brown. Remove from pans and cool on wire rack. Yield: 2 loaves.

POPPY SEED BREAD

1 c. Bisquick	1 egg, beaten
1/2 c. milk	1/4 tsp. salt
8 oz. cream cheese	Poppy seed

Mix Bisquick and milk. Spread mixture on greased pan. For the topping, mix cream cheese, beaten egg and salt. Spread mixture on top of bread mix; sprinkle with poppy seed. Bake at 400°F for 20 minutes

CHEESE BISCUITS

1 c. plain flour, sifted
¼ tsp. red pepper
½ tsp. salt

1 stick softened oleo or butter
½ lb. grated sharp cheese
1 Tbsp. Worcestershire sauce

Blend butter and cheese; add other ingredients and drop on ungreased cookie sheet. Cook at 350°F for 15-20 minutes. Yield: Makes about 30. (Drop in bite size.)

ONION-CHEESE BREAD

1½ c. milk
3 c. all-purpose flour
1 Tbsp. baking powder
1 egg beaten
½ tsp. salt

1 Tbsp. instant minced onion
¾ c. shredded sharp Cheddar cheese
3 Tbsp. melted butter or margarine
¼ tsp. pepper

Combine milk and onion in small mixing bowl; mix well and let stand 10 minutes; combine dry ingredients in a large mixing bowl. Add egg, cheese butter and milk mixture; stir only to moisten. Spread batter evenly in a greased and floured 13x9x2 inch baking pan. Bake at 375°F for 45 minutes or until lightly browned. Yield: 15 servings.

CRANBERRY BREAD

2 c. flour
¾ c. sugar
1½ tsp. baking powder
½ tsp. soda
¾ c. orange juice
1 tsp. orange zest

2 Tbsp. honey
1 egg, well beaten
2 Tbsp. vegetable oil
½ c. chopped nuts
2 c. raw cranberries, slightly chopped
   in food processor

Sift dry ingredients. Combine juice and zest; add beaten egg and oil; add dry ingredients and mix until dampened; add nuts and cranberries. Bake in loaf pan in 325°F oven for 50 to 60 minutes. Cool before slicing.

Notes

CANDIES
AND
COOKIES

DIVINITY

2½ c. sugar
½ c. water
2 egg whites
1 tsp. vanilla

½ c. white corn syrup
1 c. chopped nuts
15 small marshmallows

In heavy 2 quart saucepan mix sugar and syrup; add water; cook, stirring until sugar dissolves; boil to 267-270°F or until a small amount forms a hard ball when dropped in cold water. Gradually pour hot syrup into egg whites and marshmallows while beating at high speed (about 5 minutes); add vanilla, beat until almost hard; add nuts. Dip tablespoonfuls onto wax paper or cookie sheet. Yield: 2 dozen.

CHOCOLATE FUDGE

2 c. sugar
2 Tbsp. Karo syrup
1 Tbsp. butter
1 c. chopped pecans

3 heaping Tbsp. cocoa
⅔ c. evaporated milk
1 tsp. vanilla

In large saucepan combine sugar, evaporated milk, cocoa and Karo and bring to boil (do not stir mixture after it starts boiling); boil to 234-238°F or until a small amount forms a soft ball when dropped in cold water; set off stove into a pan of cold water; add butter and vanilla; let stand about 10 minutes, until mixture begins to thicken; add pecans and pour into buttered 8x8 inch Pyrex dish. Cool and cut into squares. Yield: about 24 squares.

DATE NUT LOAF

2 c. sugar   1 c. chopped nuts
1 c. milk   8 oz. box chopped dates
2 Tbsp. butter

Combine sugar, milk and butter in saucepan; bring to boil stirring constantly; boil slowly to 238-245°F or until a small amount dropped in cold water will form a semi-firm ball; remove from heat; add nuts and dates; stir until mixture thickens. Pour on a wet towel or cloth and form into a roll about 2 inches thick; roll up in towel and allow to cool enough to be cut. Yield: 2 dozen.

PEANUT BRITTLE

2 c. sugar   ¾ c. white Karo syrup
¼ c. water   2 c. raw peanuts
1 Tbsp. baking soda

Put all ingredients in a large heavy saucepan. Cook over low heat until peanuts are done (turning brown and popping). Add a dash of salt if desired. Remove from heat and add baking soda. STIR QUICKLY!!! Pour in a greased 11x14 inch cookie sheet. Let cool, turn over, bump and eat. Yield: 2 dozen small pieces.

Temperature: Hard crack (285-290°F).

PRALINES

1 c. brown sugar   1½ c. pecan halves
1 c. white sugar   ½ tsp. baking soda
⅓ c. Karo syrup   ½ c. cream
                               1 Tbsp. butter

Boil Karo, sugar and cream together until it reaches 234-238°F or a little dropped in cold water forms a soft ball; remove from heat; add baking soda and beat until creamy; add pecans and drop from spoon onto buttered cookie sheet or aluminum foil. Yield: 1½ dozen.

MARSHMALLOW FUDGE

3 c. sugar	1 (12 oz.) pkg. semi-sweet
¾ c. butter	chocolate pieces
1 c. chopped nuts	1 (7 oz.) jar marshmallow creme
1 tsp. vanilla	⅔ c. evaporated milk

Combine sugar, butter and milk in a 2½-quart saucepan; bring to a full rolling boil, stirring constantly. Continue boiling 5 minutes over medium heat, stirring constantly to prevent scorching. Remove from heat; stir in chocolate pieces until melted. Add marshmallow creme, nuts, and vanilla; beat until well blended. Pour into greased 13x9-inch pan. Cool at room temperature; cut into squares. Yield: approximately 3 pounds.

POPPYCOCK - CARAMEL CORN

4 c. popped corn	½ c. butter
½ c. almonds	¼ c. light corn syrup
½ c. pecans	⅔ c. sugar
1 tsp. vanilla	

Combine popped corn and nuts; spread on an ungreased baking sheet; melt butter and stir in corn syrup and sugar; bring to a boil, stirring constantly; continue boiling for 10-15 minutes stirring occasionally. When mixture turns a light caramel color, remove from heat and stir in vanilla. Pour over corn and nuts and mix until all pieces are coated. Spread out to dry. Break into pieces and store in a covered container. Yield: about 1 pound.

OATMEAL COOKIES

1 c. flour	½ c. brown sugar
½ tsp. salt	½ c. shortening
½ tsp. baking soda	½ tsp. baking powder
1 tsp. water	½ c. granulated sugar
1 tsp. vanilla	1½ c. oatmeal
1 egg	

Sift flour, salt, baking powder and soda together; add all other ingredients (except oatmeal); beat until smooth, approximately 2 minutes; fold in oats. Shape into small balls and place 1 inch apart on greased cookie sheet. Bake at 325°F for 12-15 minutes. Yield: 2½-3 dozen.

AMISH PEANUT BUTTER COOKIES

1 tsp. salt	5 c. all-purpose flour
4 eggs	1 Tbsp. baking powder
1 Tbsp. baking soda	4 tsp. vanilla extract
2 c. granulated sugar	1½ c. solid vegetable shortening
2 c. dark brown sugar, packed	1 (18 oz.) jar peanut butter,
Granulated sugar for garnish	(2 generous cups)

Preheat oven to 375°F. In a small bowl beat the eggs. In a large mixing bowl, mix together flour, salt, baking soda and baking powder; set aside. In a small mixing bowl, beat the shortening briefly, then gradually beat in the peanut butter, then sugar; blend well; add the beaten eggs a bit at a time; gradually add flour mixture and incorporate thoroughly. The batter will be very crumbly. Place garnishing sugar in a small bowl. Using a heaping tablespoon dip out batter; lightly roll a cookie in the sugar; transfer cookie to an ungreased cookie sheet. With a fork, press each cookie down a bit in a crisscross pattern to flatten. Bake 10-11 minutes or until brown. Remove from the oven and allow to cool on the sheet. Yield: 8 dozen.

CHOCOLATE CHIP COOKIES

¾ c. granulated sugar
1 tsp. baking soda
1 tsp. vanilla extract
2 eggs
½ c. cocoa

2¼ c. all-purpose flour
¾ c. packed light brown sugar
2 sticks butter, softened
2 c. (12 oz. pkg.) semi-sweet
   chocolate chips
1 c. chopped nuts (optional)

Heat oven to 375°F. Stir together flour, cocoa and baking soda. In large bowl, beat butter, granulated sugar, brown sugar and vanilla on medium speed until creamy; add eggs and beat well. Gradually add flour mixture, beating well; stir in chocolate chips and nuts. Drop rounded teaspoons onto ungreased cookie sheet. Bake 8-10 minutes or until set; cool slightly and remove from cookie sheet to wire rack. Yield: about 5 dozen cookies.

HOLIDAY COOKIES

2 c. pecans, chopped
15 oz. golden raisins
1 tsp. baking soda
1 tsp. cinnamon
1 tsp. nutmeg
1 tsp. ground cloves
4 eggs
3 Tbsp. milk

1 lb. red candied cherries, chopped
1 lb. green candied cherries, chopped
1 lb. candied pineapple, chopped
3 c. all-purpose flour
½ c. butter, softened
½ c. brown sugar, firmly packed
½ c. Amaretto

In a large bowl combine cherries, pineapple, pecans, raisins and ½ cup flour; toss mixture well to coat fruits and nuts; set aside. In a small bowl mix remaining flour, soda, cinnamon, nutmeg and cloves; set aside. In mixer cream butter; gradually adding brown sugar, beating until fluffy; add eggs one at a time beating well after each addition; add flour mixture, Amaretto and milk; mix well; pour egg mixture over fruit and mix well.

Drop dough by tablespoon full onto lightly greased cookie sheet; bake at 300°F for 20 minutes; remove from oven and cool. Yield: 9 dozen.

CHOCOLATE CHIP
PEANUT BUTTER COOKIES

½ c. butter, softened
½ c. shortening
2 eggs
1½ tsp. baking soda
1 tsp. baking powder

1 c. creamy peanut butter
1 c. light brown sugar, packed
1 c. granulated sugar
2½ c. all-purpose flour
2 c. (12 oz. pkg.) semi-sweet
chocolate chips

Heat oven to 375°F. In large bowl, beat butter, shortening, peanut butter, granulated sugar, brown sugar and eggs on medium speed until well blended. Stir together flour, baking powder and baking soda; add to butter mixture, beating until well blended. Stir in chocolate chips. Drop by tablespoon onto ungreased cookie sheet. Bake 8-10 minutes or until set. Cool slightly; remove to wire rack. Yield: about 6 dozen cookies.

CHOCOLATE PEANUT BUTTER COOKIES

1 egg
1 c. chunky peanut
butter

1 can chocolate fudge frosting
1¼ c. all-purpose flour

In large bowl, combine frosting, peanut butter and egg; blend well. Fold in flour; shape dough into 1-inch balls. Place 2 inches apart on greased cookie sheets. Flatten each with fork to 2-inch diameter. Bake at 375°F for 4 to 7 minutes or until set. DO NOT OVERBAKE. Cool 1 minute; remove from cookie sheets. Cool completely. Yield: 4 dozen cookies.

SWEET POTATO AND MOLASSES COOKIES

½ c. butter
½ c. sugar
1 egg
½ c. molasses
½ tsp. cinnamon
½ tsp. ginger

1 c. grated, raw sweet potatoes
2 c. all-purpose flour
½ tsp. baking soda
1 tsp. baking powder
¼ c. milk

Cream together butter and sugar; add egg and beat thoroughly. Blend in molasses and sweet potatoes; add the dry ingredients and milk; mix thoroughly. Drop from a teaspoon 2 inches apart on a well greased baking sheet. Bake at 375°F for 12-15 minutes or until set and lightly brown. Yield: 3-3½ dozen.

OATMEAL NUT COOKIES

1 c. butter
2 c. oatmeal
2 eggs
1 c. brown sugar
1 c. white sugar

½ tsp. vanilla extract
½ tsp. almond extract
2 c. all-purpose flour
1 tsp. baking soda
1 c. chopped nuts

Cream butter and sugars; add eggs and extracts; beat thoroughly; add flour, baking soda, and oatmeal; mix well; fold in nuts. Drop from a tablespoon 2 inches apart on a well greased baking sheet. Bake at 350°F for 12-15 minutes or until set and lightly brown. Yield: 3½-4 dozen.

TEA CAKES

½ c. butter
1 c. sugar
2 eggs

2¾ c. flour
2 tsp. baking powder
1 tsp. vanilla

Cream butter, sugar and eggs; add vanilla; add flour and baking powder. Spoon onto greased cookie sheet with a tablespoon and bake at 350°F for 10-12 minutes. Yield: 3-3½ dozen.

Notes

CASSEROLES
&
VEGETABLES

STUFFED MIRLITONS
(Chayote Squash)

4 large mirliton	1 lb. medium shrimp, peeled
1 c. celery, chopped	1 c. bell pepper, chopped
2 chopped garlic cloves	1 large onion, chopped
1 Tbsp. dry white wine	1¼ c. Italian bread crumbs, divided
1 tsp. hot sauce	1¼ c. shredded Parmesan cheese,
½ tsp. salt	divided
½ tsp. pepper	Fresh chopped chives

Garnish: Fresh chopped chives.

Boil mirlitons approximately 20 minutes; drain and cool; cut in half; scoop out pulp, leaving a ¼ inch thick shell; chop pulp and set aside.

Sauté shrimp, onion, celery, bell pepper and garlic 4-5 minutes or until shrimp turn pink; remove from heat; stir in mirliton pulp, 1 cup bread crumbs, 1 cup Parmesan cheese, wine, hot sauce, salt and pepper; stuff evenly into mirliton shells; sprinkle evenly with remaining Parmesan cheese and bread crumbs; place in a lightly greased 9x13 inch baking dish. Bake at 350°F for 30 minutes. Garnish with fresh chopped chives. Yield: 8 servings.

SAUSAGE & SHRIMP JAMBALAYA

2 cloves garlic, minced	1 lb. skinless pork link sausage
2 bay leaves	½ lb. thick sliced bacon cut into
1 tsp. salt	pieces
¼ tsp. thyme	1 lb. shrimp, peeled
½ c. minced parsley	⅛ tsp. cayenne pepper
3 large onions, chopped	1 green pepper, chopped
1⅓ c. rice	

Fry sausage and bacon, stirring frequently; remove and drain all but 2 tablespoons of fat; add onions and green pepper; cook 8-10 minutes. Add parsley, bacon, sausage, garlic and seasonings; mix well. Place shrimp over mixture, do not stir. Pour rice over shrimp; add water to barely cover rice; cover; bring to boil; reduce heat and cook 30 minutes. Remove cover, reduce heat and continue heating 15 minutes to dry jambalaya. Yield: 8 servings.

GRILLED EGGPLANT

Slice in the round in ½-inch slices; marinate for 1 hour in oil and vinegar and seasoning; grill on top rack (or cool side of grill), brushing on marinade after turning.

EASY CHICKEN DUMPLINGS

1 whole fryer	2 qts. water
1-8 oz. pkg. wide egg noodles	3 Tbsp. flour
1 can chicken broth	1 pkg. cream of chicken Cup of Soup
Salt & pepper to taste	

Wash, pat dry and season fryer; boil in 4 qt. saucepan for approximately 45 minutes, or until tender; add water as needed; remove chicken for cooling, deboning and chopping. Cook noodles in 1 can broth, adding broth from chicken. When noodles are done (approximately 6 to 8 minutes). Mix 3 Tbsp. flour in ¾ c. cooled broth (use pinch of salt and pepper in flour to help mix), add to noodles; mix 1 pkg. cream of chicken Cup of Soup in ¾ c. hot broth add to noodles; spoon chopped chicken into noodles; gently stir and simmer for about 5 minutes .Yield: 8 servings.

ROASTED CORN ON THE COB

Pull shuck back and remove silks, wash, partially dry and replace shuck; place corn in pan and roast in preheated 350°F oven for approximately 30-40 minutes. You may also grill the corn in the shuck (on top rack or cool side of grill).

CHICKEN & DUMPLINGS

3 to 4 c. flour	1 c. shortening
1 tsp. salt	1 c. milk
2 Tbsp. butter	Ice water to consistency

Chop shortening into flour & salt until coarse cornmeal consistency; work water into flour; knead; roll out thin (on floured surface); cut in 2 inch squares; let rest for 20 minutes.

Stew 2 chickens until done; cool, debone and chop. Layer chicken and dumplings alternately, ending with dumplings to make crust; dot with butter; add 1 c. milk and ½ c. chicken stock. Bake in preheated 375°F oven for 20-30 minutes.

HINT: Dumplings may be frozen by placing on waxed paper lined cookie sheet: when frozen, bag and return to freezer.
Yield: 6-8 servings.

BROCCOLI CASSEROLE

1 c. sour cream	1 pkg. (10 oz.) chopped frozen broccoli
2 eggs	1 can cream of mushroom soup
Crushed potato chips	1½ c. grated cheddar cheese

Cook broccoli as directed on package, drain. Combine soup, eggs, sour cream and cheese, mix well. Pour into buttered casserole and bake at 350°F for 20-30 minutes, or until set. Remove from oven, cover with chips and bake until light brown. Yield: 4 servings.

CAJUN CORNBREAD DRESSING

½ lb. hot sausage (bulk)	¼ c. bell pepper, finely chopped
½ lb. mild sausage (bulk)	1 c. celery, finely chopped
1 small can evaporated milk	2 bunches shallots, chopped
1 can mushroom soup	1 clove garlic, minced
1 can chicken broth	2 pkg. cornbread mix, cook in large
Salt and pepper to taste	skillet per directions

In heavy saucepan brown sausage; add peppers, shallots, celery, garlic and sauté; add crumbled cornbread, mushroom soup, evaporated milk, chicken broth, and season to taste; mix throughly. Pour into lightly greased baking pan; bake in preheated oven 350°F for 30 minutes or until done. Yield: 8 servings.

SAUSAGE & RICE CASSEROLE

1 c. uncooked rice	1 lb. hot sausage (bulk)
1 medium onion, chopped	1 can cream of mushroom soup
½ c. celery, chopped	1 can cream of chicken soup
½ c. green pepper, chopped	

Brown sausage with onion, celery and green pepper; place in baking dish with rice; add soups; bake at 350°F for 1 hour and 15 minutes, or until done; stir occasionally. Yield: 6 servings.

STUFFED ARTICHOKES

6 small artichokes	2 cloves garlic, minced
1/3 c. olive oil	2 c. French bread crumbs
1/4 tsp. salt	1/2 c. grated Parmesan cheese
1/4 tsp. pepper	3 Tbsp. chopped parsley
1/4 tsp. hot sauce	

Trim stem of each artichoke, leaving 1/2 inch; remove any damaged or tough lower leaves and trim upper edges of remaining leaves; with palm of hand, gently press down on artichoke to open up or separate leaves; wash artichokes in cold running water. Heat oil over medium heat; add garlic and cook 2 minutes, stirring constantly; remove from heat; stir in crumbs, cheese, parsley, salt, pepper and hot sauce. Stuff each leaf with crumb-cheese mixture; place artichokes in a large sauce pan and steam in 2 inches water over low heat 1 hour or until leaves can be removed easily. During steaming period, occasionally baste artichokes with additional olive oil. Yield: 6 servings

VEGETARIAN BROWN RICE

1 c. brown rice	1 Tbsp. oil or chicken stock
1/2 c. chopped onion	1/2 c chopped green pepper
2 c. sliced zucchini	3 small tomatoes, cut in 1/8s
1 crushed garlic clove	2 3/4 cups boiling chicken stock

Sauté rice in oil or chicken stock until golden, 5-10 minutes. Spoon into 2 1/2 qt. casserole; layer onion, green pepper, zucchini and tomatoes over rice; add garlic to broth; pour over vegetables. Cover and bake at 350°F for 1 hour and 15 minutes, or until liquid is absorbed and vegetables are tender. Yield: 6-8 servings.

SHRIMP & EGGPLANT CASSEROLE

1 large eggplant	1 lb. peeled shrimp
½ c. chopped peppers	½ c. chopped celery
½ c. chopped onion	8 slices stale bread, (French)
2 eggs	1 clove garlic, minced
1 c. grated cheddar cheese	

Peel eggplant; cut into small pieces; boil in a small amount of salted water until tender. Soak bread in liquid and add to cut eggplant. Sauté onion, pepper, celery, garlic and shrimp until tender but not brown. Add to the eggplant and bread mixture; add 2 beaten eggs and mix well; add salt and pepper. Put in large baking dish; top with cheese; bake for ½ hour at 350°F. Yield: 4-6 servings.

ACAPULCO BEAN CASSEROLE

1 c. chopped celery	1 (15 oz.) can chili with beans
½ c. chopped onion	1 (8¾ oz.) can whole kernel corn
2 Tbsp. butter	drained
⅛ tsp. salt	2 (3 oz.) cans jalapeño bean dip
6 corn tortillas, torn	½ c. (2 oz.) shredded sharp cheddar
1 pkg. taco seasoning mix	cheese

In saucepan cook celery and onion in butter until tender, about 10 minutes; stir in chili with beans, drained corn, taco seasoning, jalapeño bean dip and salt. Arrange half the torn tortillas in an 8x1½ inch round baking dish; top with half the chili mixture; repeat layer using remaining tortillas and chili mixture. Bake at 350°F for 35-40 minutes. Sprinkle with shredded cheese; bake uncovered until cheese melts, 2-3 minutes. Yield: 4 servings.

CANDIED SWEET POTATOES

⅓ c. honey   4 medium large sweet potatoes
⅓ c. syrup   ⅓ stick butter, melted
¼ c. Amaretto

Microwave sweet potatoes on high in covered bowl in about 1 inch of water for 30-45 minutes or until done; test with icepick. Cool, peel and chop. Place in casserole; add butter; pour honey and syrup over potatoes; drizzle with Amaretto. Bake at 350°F for 30-40 minutes or until bubbly. Yield: 6-8 servings.

RED BEANS & RICE
(Can substitute Pinto Beans)

2 lb. dried red kidney beans   1 lb. cubed ham, salt pork or smoked
½ bell pepper, chopped   sausage
2 chopped medium onions   1 tsp. salt
3 minced garlic cloves   ½ tsp. pepper
1 Tbsp. chopped parsley   Dash (¼ tsp.) Tabasco Sauce
½ tsp. thyme   2 whole bay leaves

Soak kidney beans overnight in refrigerator; drain beans and place in 5 qt. Dutch oven along with all other ingredients; add enough cold water to cover all ingredients and heat to a slow simmer, stirring frequently. Cook 1½ hours and add more water if needed; cook an additional hour after adding water or slow cook in crock pot. Serve over rice and enjoy. Yield:12-14 servings.

SKILLET SWEET POTATOES

½ c. bacon drippings   4 medium large sweet potatoes

Microwave sweet potatoes on high in covered bowl in about 1 inch of water for 12-15 minutes or until half done; test with icepick. Cool and refrigerate over night. Peel and slice lengthwise in ¼ inch slices. Fry in bacon drippings. Delicious for breakfast too! Yield: 6-8 servings.

ASPARAGUS CASSEROLE

1 c. chopped onion
¼ c. butter
1 Tbsp. butter, melted
1 c. milk
½ tsp. salt
1½ tsp. lemon juice
¼ c. chopped pimento
Dash of pepper

2 (8 oz.) pkg. frozen cut asparagus, cooked & drained
4 c. fresh mushrooms, halved
2 Tbsp. all-purpose flour
1 tsp. instant chicken bouillon granules
¾ c. soft bread crumbs (1 slice)

In covered saucepan cook mushrooms and onions in ¼ c. butter for 10 minutes or until tender; remove vegetables and set aside, leaving butter in saucepan; blend flour, chicken bouillon granules, salt, dash of pepper and return to saucepan; add milk all at once; cook and stir until bubbly; stir in mushrooms and onion, cooked asparagus, pimento and lemon juice. Turn into a 1½ quart casserole. Combine crumbs and melted butter; sprinkle on top. Bake at 350°F for 35-40 minutes. Yield: 8-10 servings.

BROCCOLI SOUFFLÉ

2 Tbsp. butter	2 c. chopped broccoli or
½ tsp. salt	(1 pkg, 10 oz. frozen chopped)
4 eggs, divided	2 Tbsp. all-purpose flour
½ c. milk	¼ c. grated Parmesan cheese

In covered saucepan cook fresh chopped broccoli in boiling water for 8-10 minutes (per directions if frozen); drain well; chop any large pieces. In saucepan melt butter; blend in flour and salt; add milk all at once; cook and stir until bubbly; remove from heat. Beat egg yolks until thick and lemon colored (with electric mixer); slowly stir half of the hot mixture into yolks; return to remaining hot mixture; stir rapidly; stir in cheese and broccoli; wash beaters; beat egg whites until stiff peaks form; fold into broccoli mixture. Turn into an ungreased 1 quart soufflé dish. Bake at 350°F for 35-40 minutes or until knife inserted in center comes out clean. Yield: 4 servings.

MIRLITON (SQUASH) CASSEROLE

1 pkg. dressing mix	3 c. cooked mirliton, or (2 cans squash,
1 onion chopped	drained)
½ stick butter	1 can cream of mushroom soup
4 oz. sour cream	½ tsp. Creole seasoning
½ c. chopped parsley	

Melt butter and mix with dressing mix and other ingredients; pour into casserole dish and bake at 325°F for 30 minutes. Yield: 6-8 servings.

GREEN BEAN CASSEROLE

2 cans green beans	1 can cream of mushroom soup
½ c. cheddar cheese, grated	1 c. french fried onion rings
¼ c. bacon bits	1 c. sliced water chestnuts
1 c. liquid from beans	1 small can sliced mushrooms

Mix all ingredients except onion rings and cheese; place in a 1½ quart casserole; cook at 350°F for 30 minutes. Top with cheese and crushed onion rings. Heat in oven another 5 minutes. Yield: 4-6 servings.

SHRIMP FETTUCCINI

¼ c. vegetable oil	1 8 oz. pkg. fettuccini pasta
6 Tbsp. butter	1 lb. small shrimp, peeled & de-veined
3 Tbsp. chopped parsley	1 c. grated Romano cheese
1 c. heavy cream	Salt & white pepper to taste

Cook fettuccini in salted, boiling water, do not over cook. Drain; rinse with cold water; toss with vegetable oil. In a medium pan melt butter and add cream and shrimp and cook over low heat until pink. Add fettuccini, cheese, salt, white pepper and parsley; toss to coat well; remove from heat. Serve immediately. Yield: 4 servings.

BROCCOLI & RICE CASSEROLE

1 c. cooked rice	1 (10 oz.) pkg frozen chopped broccoli
1 c. chopped onion	1 (10 oz.) can cream of mushroom
1 c. chopped celery	1 (8 oz.) jar pasteurized processed
1 Tbsp. oil	cheese spread
1¼ c. milk	Dash or 2 or more of Tabasco

Cook broccoli according to package directions; drain and set aside. Sauté onions and celery in oil until transparent; add mushroom soup, milk, cheese and Tabasco and stir until cheese is melted. Blend in rice and broccoli.

Transfer mixture to a baking dish or casserole, top with bread crumbs and a few slivered almonds, if desired, and bake at 300°F for 30 minutes or until slightly browned. Yield: 6 servings.

BROCCOLI CASSEROLE

2 Tbsp. grated onion	1 pkg. frozen chopped broccoli
2 eggs	1 can mushroom soup
¼ c. mayonnaise	1 c. grated sharp cheese
Salt and pepper	½ c. sour cream
Buttered bread crumbs	

Cook broccoli and drain; combine other ingredients; add broccoli; pour into greased casserole dish; top with bread crumbs; bake at 400°F until firm, about 25 minutes. Cut into squares for serving. Yield: 6 servings.

CORN & SAUSAGE CASSEROLE

¾ lb. pork sausage   2 cans well drained kernel corn
2 Tbsp. flour   ¼ c. chopped green pepper
½ tsp. salt   6 tomato slices
½ c. grated American cheese   1½ c. undiluted evaporated milk

Brown sausage and pepper over medium heat until pork is cooked; add to corn in buttered 1½ quart casserole; blend 2 Tbsp. of meat drippings with flour and salt over medium heat; slowly add milk; simmer 2-3 minutes or until thickened; stirring occasionally; pour over casserole; top with grated cheese and tomato slices; bake in moderate oven, 350°F, 25-30 minutes. Yield: 6-8 servings.

PORK FRIED RICE

3-4 Tbsp. soy sauce   1 (14½ oz.) can peas and carrots,
1 onion, finely chopped   drained
2 Tbsp. vegetable oil   3 green onions, sliced
7-8 c. cooked rice   4 cooked pork chops, diced

In large skillet or wok, cook chopped onion in hot oil until tender-crisp; add cooked rice; cook over medium heat 8 minutes or until heated through, stirring frequently; stir in meat, vegetables and soy sauce; heat through; season with pepper if desired. Yield: 4 servings.

PECAN WILD RICE PILAF

4 c. chicken broth	1 c. wild rice, well rinsed
1¾ c. wheat pilaf	1 bunch scallions, thinly sliced
1 c. pecan halves	½ c. chopped Italian parsley
1 c. dried currants	Grated zest of 2 oranges
2 Tbsp. olive oil	½ c. chopped fresh mint leaves
Black pepper	1 Tbsp. orange juice

In a medium saucepan bring the broth to a boil; add wild rice and bring back to boil; reduce heat to medium-low and cook covered for 50 minutes or until tender; do not overcook; remove to a large bowl. In another saucepan bring 2¼ c. water to boil; add pilaff; reduce heat to low and simmer 15 minutes or until pilaf is tender; remove from heat, let rest 15 minutes, then add to rice. Add remaining ingredients and toss well. Serve at room temperature. Yield: 8 servings.

SPINACH & ARTICHOKE CASSEROLE

1 stick butter	2 pkg. frozen chopped spinach
1 (8 oz.) pkg. cream cheese	1 can water chestnuts, sliced
¼ c. Italian bread crumbs	2 cans artichoke bottoms, save liquid

Cook spinach per directions and drain; grease bottom of 9x12x2 inch pan with a little olive oil; put artichoke bottoms in pan. Melt butter and break up cheese in butter and blend as well as possible; add bread crumbs and blend; add spinach and water chestnuts; add water (or artichoke juice) to moisten. Put mixture over artichokes; top with bread crumbs and sprinkle a little olive oil on top. Bake 30 minutes in 350°F oven or until brown on top. Yield: 8 servings.

SEAFOOD STUFFED EGGPLANT

6 medium eggplants	½ lb. small shrimp
½ lb. crabmeat	2 bell peppers, chopped
¼ c. chopped parsley	1 pod (5 cloves) minced garlic
¼ c. chopped celery	2 medium onions, chopped
Bread crumbs	Salt and pepper to taste

Peel and cube eggplants; boil until tender. Sauté peppers, onion, parsley, garlic and celery until limp; add eggplant; smother until water is gone; add shrimp; cook 20 minutes. Add crabmeat, salt and pepper; mix; put in baking dish; sprinkle with bread crumbs and butter on top. Bake at 350°F until brown. Yield: 6-8 servings.

CRABMEAT AU GRATIN

1 lb. white or lump crabmeat	2 egg yolks, well beaten
½ stick butter	1 tsp. salt
1 c. onion, chopped fine	½ tsp. red pepper
1 stalk celery, chopped fine	¼ tsp. black pepper
2 cloves garlic, chopped fine	Dash Worcestershire sauce
1 bell pepper, chopped fine	1 small jar mushrooms
¼ c. all-purpose flour	¼ c. cheddar cheese, grated
2 c. whole milk	

Sauté vegetables in butter until well done, but not brown; add mushrooms; blend flour into mixture; pour in milk gradually, stirring constantly. Add egg yolks, salt, red & black peppers; cool for 5 minutes. Add crabmeat and Worcestershire to sauce; blend well and transfer into lightly greased casserole dish. Sprinkle top with cheese and bake at 350°F for 15-20 minutes. Yield: 4-6 servings.

ARNAUD'S CRABMEAT MONACO

4 lbs. crabmeat	6 Tbsp. shallots, chopped
1 lb. mushrooms	2 Tbsp. sugar
1 lb. diced tomatos	2 c. red wine
½ c. tomato paste	4 pinches each of salt & pepper
2 Tbsp. garlic, chopped	Bread crumbs & grated cheese

Boil wine for 7 minutes. At the same time sauté garlic, mushrooms, tomatoes and green onions until they are brown; add crabmeat, tomato paste, salt and pepper, sugar and wine. Cook for 15 minutes; place in ramekins; top with bread crumbs and grated cheese; heat until brown. Yield: 10 servings.

SWEET & SOUR BAKED BEANS

8 slices bacon	½ c. brown sugar, packed
4 onions, sliced	2 (15 oz.) cans butter beans
1 tsp. mustard	1 (1 lb.) can green lima beans
1 tsp. salt	1 (1 lb.) can red kidney beans
½ tsp. garlic powder	1 (1 lb.) can baked beans
½ c. apple cider vinegar	

Fry bacon in skillet until crisp; remove from pan; drain on paper toweling; crumble and set aside. Separate onion slices into rings; cook in bacon drippings until tender but not browned. Stir in salt, sugar, mustard, garlic powder and vinegar; cover and simmer 20 minutes. Drain butter, lima and kidney beans; mix all beans with onion mixture and bacon and turn into 3 quart casserole. Bake for 1 hour at 350°F. Yield: 12-14 servings.

DILLED CABBAGE

6-8 Tbsp. water
4-6 Tbsp. Italian dressing
½ tsp. chopped dill or to taste

½ large head cabbage, thinly sliced
4 cherry tomatoes, halved

In skillet combine cabbage with dill; let stand 5-10 minutes. Add dressing and water; stir fry over medium heat until cabbage is tender-crisp; add additional water if desired. Garnish with halved tomatoes. Yield: 4 servings.

FRIED GREEN TOMATOES

¼ c. cornmeal
¼ c. Bisquick
Salt & pepper to taste

3 large, firm green tomatoes
Bacon drippings or shortening

Cut tomatoes into ¼-inch slices. Season with salt and pepper; mix cornmeal and Bisquick and dredge tomatoes in mix. Heat bacon drippings in a heavy skillet; add tomatoes, and fry slowly until browned, turning once. Yield: 4 servings.

CORN SOUFFLÉ

4 eggs, beaten
2 Tbsp. flour
4 Tbsp. butter
Salt and pepper

2 (15¼ oz.) cans whole kernel corn
   drained
2 (15¼ oz.) cans cream style corn

Beat eggs and stir into corn; add flour and salt and pepper to taste. Put into casserole; add butter and break up. Bake at 350°F for 30-45 minutes, until bubbly in the middle and starting to form crust around the edges. Yield: 8 servings.

CREOLE JAMBALAYA

1 c. chopped onions	1 lb. smoked ham, cubed
½ c. chopped green pepper	½ lb. hot sausage, chopped
¼ c. chopped green onions	½ lb. smoked sausage, chopped
1 tsp. chopped garlic	1 lb. shrimp (peeled & de-veined)
1 Tbsp. chopped parsley	1 tsp. ground thyme
3 c. uncooked rice	1 bay leaf
4 c. boiling water	½ tsp. Creole seasoning
½ tsp. salt	

Place ham, sausages, onions and pepper in 3-quart saucepan; cover and cook over medium heat until onions are soft; add rice and stir well; add all other ingredients; bring to boil. Let boil for 5 minutes; lower heat; cover pot tightly and let cook slowly for 35 minutes or until rice is tender. Fluff rice and mix well. Yield: 6-8 servings.

ASPARAGUS QUICHE

1 (9 in.) pastry shell	2 Tbsp. grated Parmesan cheese
6 slices bacon	6 stalks asparagus, partially cooked
1 large onion	¼ tsp. nutmeg
4 eggs	1 c. cubed Swiss cheese
2 c. heavy cream	Salt and pepper

Bake pastry shell 5 minutes. Sauté bacon until crisp. Slice onion very thin and sauté onion until transparent. Combine bacon, onion, and Swiss cheese and arrange in pastry shell. Mix cream, eggs and nutmeg; salt and pepper to taste; pour into pie; top with asparagus partly cooked; sprinkle Parmesan cheese over top; Bake at 350°F for 35-40 minutes. Yield: 6-8 servings.

EGGPLANT & BEEF SUPREME

1 medium eggplant	1 lb. ground beef
1 stick butter	1 Tbsp. instant minced onion
1 tsp. salt	⅛ tsp. black pepper
1 tsp. sugar	1 (8 oz.) can tomato sauce
¼ tsp. oregano	¼ c. grated Parmesan cheese
¼ tsp. basil leaves	½ lb. Mozzarella cheese, sliced

Cut eggplant into ½-inch slices; lightly brown eggplant slices in butter, adding extra butter if needed. Place in shallow 2-quart baking dish. To drippings in skillet, add ground beef, salt, pepper, onion, sugar, basil leaves and oregano; cook well until meat is lightly browned. Spoon meat mixture over eggplant; add tomato sauce and Parmesan cheese. Bake, uncovered, in 350°F oven for 20 minutes. Place Mozzarella cheese on top of casserole. Bake 10 minutes longer or until cheese is melted. Yield: 6 servings.

CABBAGE ROLLS

1 lb. ground chuck	3 Tbsp. onion, finely chopped
1 egg beaten	3 Tbsp. green pepper, finely chopped
½ c. uncooked rice	1 (16 oz.) can tomato sauce with claret
8 whole cabbage leaves	wine
1 Tbsp. lemon juice	1 Tbsp. Worcestershire Sauce
Salt & pepper to taste	

Combine meat, rice, onion, pepper, egg. and seasoning to taste. Scald cabbage leaves until limp; roll out meat rolls; add 1 tablespoon tomato sauce per roll before wrapping with cabbage leaf. Pour remaining sauce over cabbage rolls; cover with foil; bake at 350°F for 45 minutes. Yield: 8 servings.

FETTUCINI ALFREDO

2 Tbsp. light cream	1 (8 oz.) pkg. egg noodles
Salt & pepper to taste	½ c. grated Parmesan cheese
	1 stick butter, softened

Cook noodles according to directions. Meanwhile combine butter, cream, cheese, salt and pepper. When noodles are done, toss with cheese mixture. Serve immediately. Yield: 8 servings.

TACO QUICHE

1 egg	1 lb. chuck
Sour cream	1 (9 in.) pie crust, frozen
Shredded lettuce	1 (1¼ oz.) envelope taco seasoning
1 (16 oz.) jar Picanté sauce	1½ c. Monterey Jack cheese, shredded
Guacamole or avocados	and divided
	1 (4½ oz.) can chopped green chilies

In skillet brown beef and drain; add taco seasoning and 1 cup Picanté sauce. Simmer for 5-8 minutes; remove from heat; stir in egg. Sprinkle pie crust with ½ cup cheese; top with green chilies. Pour beef mixture over chilies; top with remaining cheese. Bake at 350°F on preheated baking sheet 20-25 minutes.

Serve with lettuce, sour cream, guacamole and remaining Picanté sauce. Yield: 6 servings.

SPINACH WITH SOUR CREAM

2 eggs, beaten	1 pkg. frozen chopped spinach
1 Tbsp. grated onion	1 c. grated Parmesan cheese
1 c. sour cream	1 Tbsp. flour
2 Tbsp. butter	Salt and pepper to taste

Cook spinach, onion, and salt & pepper with small amount of water until thawed; add beaten eggs, and remaining ingredients to spinach and mix well. Place in greased casserole and bake at 350°F for 25-30 minutes or until center is set. Do not overcook. Yield: 4 servings.

EGG PLANT LASAGNA

½ c. minced onion	1 (15 oz.) can tomato sauce
½ c. chopped celery	½ c. chopped green pepper
½ tsp. dried oregano	¼ lb. sliced mushrooms (optional)
½ tsp. dried basil	1 large or 2 small eggplants, thinly
¼ tsp. pepper	sliced
2 cloves minced garlic	2 Tbsp. freshly minced parsley
1 c. low fat cottage cheese	4 oz. part-skim mozzarella cheese,
	thinly sliced

In a saucepan combine tomato sauce, onion, celery, green pepper, mushrooms, oregano, basil, garlic, pepper, and parsley; cover and simmer at least one hour, stirring occasionally. In a 13x9x2 inch baking dish layer eggplant, cottage cheese, tomato sauce mixture and mozzarella cheese; repeat layers. Bake at 350°F for approximately 30 minutes. Yield: 4 servings.

Option: May also use 1 lb. browned ground chuck and 1 10 oz. pkg. lasagna noodles. Increase cooking time to approximately 45 minutes.

Notes

DESSERTS
AND
CAKES

MARBLE CHIFFON CAKE

⅓ c. baking cocoa
¼ c. boiling water
1 Tbsp. baking powder
¾ c. water
½ tsp. cream of tartar
7 eggs, separated

1½ c. plus 3 Tbsp. sugar, divided
½ c. plus 2 Tbsp. vegetable oil,
    divided
2¼ c. all-purpose flour
2 Tbsp. grated orange peel

ORANGE GLAZE:
3-4 Tbsp. orange juice
½ tsp. grated orange peel

2 c. confectioners sugar
⅓ butter, melted

In a bowl, combine cocoa, boiling water, 3 Tbsp. sugar and 2 Tbsp. oil; whisk until smooth; cool. In a mixing bowl, combine flour, baking powder and remaining sugar. Whisk egg yolks, ¾ c. water and remaining oil; add to dry ingredients. Beat until well blended. Beat egg whites and cream of tartar until soft peaks form; fold into batter. Remove 2 cups of batter; stir into cocoa mixture. To the remaining batter, add orange peel. Alternately spoon the batters into an ungreased 10-inch tube pan. Swirl with a knife. Bake at 325°F for 70-75 minutes or until top springs back when lightly touched. Invert cake pan on a wire rack; cool.

For the glaze, combine sugar, butter and enough orange juice to reach desired consistency. Add orange peel; spoon over cake.
Yield: 12-14 servings.

BUTTER CAKE

½ lb. butter or oleo (2 sticks)
5 eggs
2 tsp. vanilla

1¾ c. sugar
2 c. all-purpose flour
1 tsp. baking soda
2 tsp. baking powder

Bring butter and eggs to room temperature. In mixer cream butter and sugar; add 1 egg at a time, alternate with flour (with baking soda and powder), beat well after each adding. Bake in Bundt pan at 350°F for 45 minutes. Yield: 12 servings.

BLACK FOREST CAKE

1 c. chopped nuts
1 sm. bottle Maraschino
cherries
Chocolate curls

Use recipe for brownies. or
1 pkg. devil's food cake mix
1 (21 oz.) can cherry pie filling, divided
2½ c. whipped cream, divided

Heat oven to 350°F. Grease and flour 2 (9-inch) round cake pans; prepare brownie or devil's food cake mix; add nuts; divide batter into the 2 pans. Bake at 350°F for 18-20 minutes. Do not over-bake. Cool 10 minutes. Remove from pans to wire racks to cool completely. Place one layer on serving plate. Top with 1 c. whipped cream, spreading to within ½ inch of edge. Spread ½ cherry filling evenly over whipped cream. Repeat with second layer. Spread whipped cream over top and sides of cake; spread remaining cherry filling over top; decorate with maraschino cherries and chocolate curls. Yield: 10-12 servings.

RUM CAKE

½ c. water
½ c. vegetable oil
½ c. rum
4 eggs

1 c. pecans, chopped
1 pkg. yellow cake mix
1 pkg. french vanilla instant pudding

SAUCE:
1 stick butter
1 c. sugar

¼ c. water
2 oz. rum

Cake: Sprinkle chopped pecans on bottom of greased 10-inch tube or Bundt pan. Mix together cake mix, pudding, water, vegetable oil, and rum. Beat in eggs, one at a time. Pour batter into pan. Bake 1 hour at 325°F.

Sauce: Boil butter, sugar, water, and rum together in a saucepan. Pour over cake while in pan. This will soak into cake. Let cake cool completely before removing from pan. This freezes beautifully. Yield: 12 servings.

LEMON-AMARETTO BUNDT CAKE

1½ c. sliced almonds
5 eggs
2 c. sugar
2 c. all-purpose flour

1 Tbsp. fresh lemon juice
½ lb. butter (2 sticks), softened
1 tsp. vanilla extract
½ tsp. lemon extract
1 Tbsp. lemon zest (finely grated)

SYRUP:
4 Tbsp. Amaretto

6 Tbsp. granulated sugar
3 Tbsp. fresh lemon juice

Preheat oven to 350°F. Spread almonds on baking sheet and brown for 8-10 minutes, or until just golden. Remove and set aside.

Lightly grease and flour a 10 inch nonstick bundt pan; sprinkle ½ c. toasted almonds evenly over the bottom of pan. In an electric mixer bowl, cream butter, sugar and lemon zest until pale yellow and fluffy; add flour; stir just enough to blend; add lemon juice and extracts; stir; add eggs one at a time, stirring after each addition; gently fold in remaining toasted almonds; scrape into prepared pan and bake until cake tester inserted into center comes out clean, about 70 minutes. (After 30 minutes of baking, cover top of cake tightly with aluminum foil.)

Prepare syrup: In a sauce pan, slowly heat the sugar, Amaretto and lemon juice; stirring until sugar melts. Reserve until ready to use.

When cake is done, remove from oven; with a cake tester, poke holes all over the bottom of the cake (which is now on top). Carefully pour or brush on half of the syrup until it is absorbed into holes.

Cool cake in the pan on a cake rack for ten minutes; gently invert the cake onto another rack and remove from pan. With a cake tester poke holes into top and sides of the cake; brush with remaining syrup. You can increase the amount of liqueur to taste. Cool and serve or store. Yield: 12 servings.

CHOCOLATE-AMARETTO CHEESE CAKE

1½ c. light processed cream
cheese
1 c. 1% low-fat cottage cheese
¼ c. all-purpose flour
¾ c. sugar + 1 Tbsp.
1 tsp. vanilla extract
¼ c. Amaretto

¼ c. + 2 Tbsp. cocoa, unsweetened
6 chocolate wafers, finely crushed
1 egg
2 Tbsp. semisweet chocolate
mini-morsels
Chocolate curls (optional)

Sprinkle chocolate wafer crumbs in bottom of springform pan.
Position knife blade in food processor bowl; add cream cheese and
next 6 ingredients, processing until smooth. Add egg and process just
until blended. Fold in chocolate morsels.

Slowly pour mixture over crumbs in pan. Bake at 300°F for 65-70
minutes or until cheese cake is set. Let cool in pan on wire rack. Cover
and chill at least 8 hours. Remove sides of pan, and transfer cheese to
a serving platter. Garnish with chocolate curls, if desired.
Yield: 12 servings.

NEW ORLEANS DATE NUT BARS

6 Tbsp. butter
2 eggs
1½ tsp. baking powder
¼ tsp. ground cinnamon
¼ c. milk
¾ c. chopped nuts

¾ c. light brown sugar, firmly packed
1½ c. all-purpose flour
1 tsp. vanilla
1 (8 oz.) pkg. chopped dates
Confectioners' sugar

Beat butter and sugar together until creamy; add eggs and vanilla and
beat until blended. Combine flour, baking powder, and cinnamon.
Stir alternately with milk into sugar mixture. Fold in chopped dates
and nuts. Spread in greased 9x9x2 inch baking pan. Bake in
preheated oven at 350°F for 35 minutes or until done. Cool; dust with
confectioners sugar; cut into 3x1-inch bars. Yield: 24 bars.

CRANBERRY-ORANGE POUND CAKE

6 eggs

2½ c. sugar

3 c. all-purpose flour

1 tsp. baking powder

1 c. sour cream

1½ c. butter (3 sticks), softened

2½ tsp. grated orange peel

1½ c. chopped cranberries,
    fresh or frozen

1 tsp. vanilla extract

Cream butter and sugar until light and fluffy. Add eggs, one at a time, beating well after each addition. Stir in vanilla and orange peel. Combine flour and baking powder add to the creamed mixture alternately with sour cream; beat on low until blended; fold in cranberries. Pour into greased and floured 10-inch tube pan; bake at 350°F for 65-70 minutes or until a wooden toothpick inserted near the center comes out clean. Cool in pan for 10 minutes; remove to a wire rack and cool completely.

VANILLA BUTTER SAUCE:

1 c. sugar

½ c. butter softened

½ tsp. vanilla extract

1 tbsp. all-purpose flour

½ c. half-and-half cream

In a small saucepan, combine sugar and flour. Stir in cream and butter; bring to a boil over a medium heat, stirring constantly. Remove from the heat and stir in vanilla. Serve warm over cake.

Yield: 16 servings (1½ cups sauce)

ICE BOX FRUIT CAKE

1 c. white raisins

1 qt. pecans, chopped

14 oz. vanilla wafers,
    rolled out fine

½ lb. candied pineapple

½ lb. candied cherries

1 can condensed milk

Mix thoroughly. Line bread pan with aluminum foil and pack solid. Refrigerate, slice and serve. Yield: 15-20 servings.

APPLE CAKE

2 c. sugar	1 tsp. baking soda
1¼ c. vegetable oil	2 tsp. baking powder
3 c. all-purpose flour	2 tsp. vanilla
3 large eggs, beaten	1 c. chopped pecans
3 c. chopped raw apples	3 Tbsp. Amaretto (optional)

In a bowl, combine vegetable oil and sugar; beat at low speed until creamy; add eggs, vanilla and Amaretto. Sift baking soda, baking powder and flour together; add to oil and sugar mixture; beat until smooth; mix in pecans and apples. Preheat oven to 325°F. Pour into a greased and floured 13x9x2 inch pan. Bake 45 to 50 minutes. Let cool before removing from pan. Yield: 12 servings.

HOT BUTTERED RUM SAUCE:

1 c. sugar	½ c. light cream
1 stick butter	1 tsp. rum extract

Combine sugar, butter and cream in a saucepan and heat over low heat, stirring until hot; stir in rum extract. Spoon hot sauce over individual servings.

SOUR CREAM POUND CAKE

1 c. (2 sticks) butter	2 tsp. almond extract
2 c. sugar	1 tsp. vanilla extract
2 tsp. baking powder	2¾ c. sifted flour
1 tsp. baking soda	1 c. sour cream
5 eggs	¾ c. chopped pecans

Bring butter and eggs to room temperature; preheat oven to 325°F. In a large mixing bowl cream sugar and butter; add eggs, one at a time, beating well after each addition; add flavorings; add flour (with baking powder, baking soda) and sour cream alternately. Mix well and bake in greased and floured 10-inch tube pan for 1 hour and 15 minutes, or until cake tests done. Yield: 12-14 servings.

CHERRY NUT POUND CAKE

1 c. butter (2 sticks)	1 tsp. vanilla extract
2 c. sugar	1 tsp. almond extract
2¾ c. plain flour	2 tsp. baking powder
1 c. sour cream	1 tsp. baking soda
5 eggs	*5 oz. maraschino cherries, well
1 c. chopped pecans	drained and chopped

Cream together butter and sugar until creamy; add vanilla and almond extract; add eggs, one at a time, add flour (with baking powder, baking soda) and sour cream, beating well after each addition; fold in pecans and cherries (*use 10 oz. cherries if you are not icing cake); pour into large greased 10-inch tube pan. Place in preheated 325°F oven and bake for 1 hour and 15 minutes. Cool thoroughly and frost. Yield: 12-14 servings.

FROSTING:

½ stick butter	8 oz. cream cheese
1 tsp. vanilla extract	1 lb. confectioners sugar
1 tsp. almond extract	1 c. shredded coconut
1 c. chopped walnuts	5 oz. chopped maraschino cherries

Bring butter and cream cheese to room temperature and blend until smooth; gradually add confectioners sugar and beat until smooth; add almond and vanilla extract and mix well; fold in coconut, chopped walnuts, and maraschino cherries. Spread mixture over cake.

BROWNIES

1¾ c. sugar	⅓ c. vegetable oil
¾ c. cocoa	1 c. all-purpose flour
3 eggs, beaten	1 tsp. baking powder
1 c. chopped nuts	2 Tbsp. liquid coffee
Marshmallows	1 tsp. vanilla & 2 Tbsp. Kahlúa

Zap oil in microwave for 20 seconds, and mix with sugar, vanilla, Kahlúa and coffee; add cocoa, flour, baking powder, eggs and nuts. Preheat oven to 325°F; Grease bottom of 9x13 inch pan; spread mixture into pan; bake for 35 minutes until edges begin to pull away from pan. Cool pan on wire rack; add marshmallows and melt until golden brown; cool. Yield: 24 pieces.

MINUTE BOIL FUDGE FROSTING

½ c. sugar
7 Tbsp. milk
4 Tbsp. butter

2 oz. unsweetened chocolate cut fine
1 tsp. vanilla
1 Tbsp. corn syrup

Combine in sauce pan all ingredients except vanilla; slowly bring to a full rolling boil, stirring constantly; boil briskly for 1½ minutes. Cool to lukewarm; add vanilla and beat until thick enough to spread.

TRIFLE PUDDING

3 peeled and sliced kiwis
1½ c. chopped pecans
1 pound cake
Cool Whip
¼ c. Amaretto

3 (15¼ oz.) cans sliced peaches in heavy syrup or fresh peaches
Maraschino cherries (or fresh strawberries), chopped
2 (6 oz.) pkg. vanilla instant pudding prepared as directed

Prepare pudding and set aside. Drain peaches; save juice; mix ¼ cup juice with ¼ cup Amaretto (if fresh peaches and strawberries are used drizzle with Amaretto); cube cake and lay on bottom of bowl; drizzle cake with juice and Amaretto mixture; add layer of peaches, kiwis and cherries and sprinkle with pecans; add layer of pudding. Repeat layers and top with Cool Whip. Refrigerate. Yield: 12-15 servings.

Hint: Put leftover fresh peaches in vanilla ice cream or strawberries in chocolate ice cream in freezer.

BUTTER FROSTING

1 stick butter
1 c. chopped pecans

1 (8 oz.) pkg. cream cheese
1 pkg. confectioners sugar

Zap butter and cream cheese in microwave; whip cream cheese; add butter and sugar; fold in pecans.

BREAD PUDDING & WHISKEY SAUCE

1 qt. sweet milk	1 loaf French bread
1 c. sugar	4 eggs
1 Tbsp. vanilla	1 c. raisins
3 Tbsp. butter	

Crumble bread, soak in milk and mix well; add eggs, sugar, vanilla and raisins and stir well. Pour melted butter into bottom of baking pan or casserole and add other ingredients. Bake at 325°F for 1 hour, or until pudding is puffed and golden and knife inserted in center comes out clean. Yield: 12-15 servings.

WHISKEY SAUCE:

½ c. butter	1 egg yolk, beaten
1 c. sugar	1 small can evaporated milk
2 jiggers bourbon	

Combine butter, sugar, egg yolk and evaporated milk in top of double boiler; cook, stirring over simmering water, until thickened; stir in bourbon. Serve on warm bread pudding.

RUSSIAN CREAM

1 c. sugar	1 env. unflavored gelatin
1 c. boiling water	1 c. heavy cream
½ c. plain yogurt	½ c. sour cream
1½ tsp. vanilla	Fresh berries, (raspberries or strawberries)

Mix gelatin with sugar; add boiling water; stir until sugar is dissolved; stir in heavy cream and chill for thirty minutes. Mixture should become slightly thickened.

Remove from refrigerator; add sour cream, yogurt and vanilla; mix with electric beater at low speed.

Pour into glasses or serving bowl; refrigerate another 2 hours. Serve with fresh berries on top. Yield: 6-8 servings.

INDIVIDUAL FRUIT CAKES

3 eggs, separated	¼ c. flour (for fruits and nuts
½ c. (1 stick) butter	*¼ lb. candied lemon peel
2 c. sifted flour	*¼ lb. candied orange peel
1 tsp. cinnamon	*¼ lb. citron
1 tsp. allspice	*¼ lb. glazed cherries
1 tsp. nutmeg	*¼ lb. dates
1 tsp. baking soda	*¼ lb. candied pineapple
1 c. cane syrup	¼ lb. seedless raisins
⅓ c. fruit juice	3 c. pecans

* (or 1½ pounds mixed candied fruit)

Cream yolks and butter. Sift flour, spices and soda; add alternately with syrup and fruit juice to butter mixture. Chop fruits; flour dates, nuts and fruits; add to batter; fold in stiffly beaten egg whites. Place one tablespoon mixture into each greased muffin tin or paper soufflé cup. Bake in 250°F oven for 45 minutes.
Yield: Approximately 85 cakes.

For large cake, pour batter into greased 10-inch tube pan; bake in 275°F oven for 3¼ hours. Yield: 5 pound cake.

FUDGE FROSTING

2 Tbsp. butter	3 squares (1 oz. each) unsweetened
½ c. light cream	chocolate
1 tsp. vanilla	2¾ c. powdered sugar, sifted

Place butter and chocolate in small pyrex mixing bowl. Microwave for 2 to 3 minutes on HIGH or until melted. Combine remaining ingredients in medium mixing bowl; beat well. Slowly beat in chocolate mixture. Beat on medium speed until frosting is spreading consistency.

MARDI GRAS KING'S CAKE

1 pkg. yeast	1 c. (2 sticks) butter
¾ c. sugar	¼ c. warm water
4 eggs	4 c. sifted flour
Melted butter	6 Tbsp. milk, scalded & cooled

In a bowl, dissolve yeast in warm water; add milk and enough flour, about ½ cup, to make a soft dough. In another bowl, combine butter, sugar and eggs with electric mixer; remove from mixer and add soft ball of yeast dough; mix thoroughly. Gradually add 2½ cups flour to make a medium dough that is neither too soft nor too stiff; place in a greased bowl and brush top of dough with butter; cover with a damp cloth and set aside to rise until doubled in bulk, about 3 hours.

Use remaining 1 cup flour to knead dough and to roll with hands into a "rope" shape; place on a 14x17 inch greased cookie sheet and form "rope" of dough into an oval shape; the center should be about 7x12 inches; connect ends of dough by dampening with water; cover with a damp cloth and let rise until doubled in bulk, about 1 hour. Bake in 325°F oven for 35 to 45 minutes or until lightly browned. Decorate by brushing top of cake with corn syrup and alternating 3-inch bands of purple, green and gold colored granulated sugar. (To color sugar, add a few drops of food coloring to sugar, and shake in tightly covered jar until desired color is achieved.)

Insert Baby (or bean) through bottom of cake AFTER cooking, before decorating. The person getting the piece of cake with the baby (or bean) is the one to give the next Mardi Gras party, or provide the cake.

Note: Mardi Gras always falls on the day before Ash Wednesday. The parties start in early January.

LAZY APPLE STRUDEL

¾ c. melted butter
1 c. milk
2 egg yolks
1 c. sugar, divided
Ground cinnamon
Melted butter

3½ c. all-purpose flour
5-6 large cooking apples,
  peeled and sliced
½ c. chopped pecans, divided
½ c. flaked coconut, divided
½ c. raisins

Combine butter, milk, egg yolks and flour; blend well; chill dough at least 2 hours.

Divide dough into 2 parts; roll each part on a floured surface to a 12x18 inch rectangle. Brush surface with melted butter. Arrange half the apple slices in the center of each rectangle in a single layer, leaving a 2-inch border without apples. Sprinkle half the raisins, pecans, coconut, and sugar over apples on each rectangle. Sprinkle cinnamon over all.

Starting with long edge, roll up jellyroll fashion, turning in ends as you roll. Place strudels on a greased jellyroll pan, seam-side down. Bake at 350°F for 1 hour. Yield: 2 (14-inch) strudels.

BANANAS SUPREME

1 Tbsp. lemon juice
2 Tbsp. Amaretto
¼ c. light rum
⅓ c. brown sugar
2 Tbsp. butter

3 ripe bananas, diagonally sliced,
  ½ inch thick
½ c. heavy cream, whipped
⅓ c. coconut, toasted
⅛ tsp. nutmeg (optional)

Melt sugar and butter in 10-inch skillet; add lemon juice, nutmeg (optional), Amaretto, and rum; simmer for 2 minutes; add bananas, stir gently and saute until just tender. Divide bananas and sauce into six dessert dishes. Top with whipped cream and coconut. Yield: 6 servings.

CHOCOLATE KAHLÚA CAKE

2 c. sugar
3 c. flour
3 eggs
½ c. sour cream
2 tsp. baking powder
2 tsp. baking soda
1 tsp. vanilla

½ c. Kahlúa, divided
1 c. chopped nuts
2 sticks butter, softened
4 Tbsp. instant coffee granules
1 (8 oz.) pkg. unsweetened baking
  chocolate, melted

Bring eggs and butter to room temperature. Melt chocolate and mix in coffee granules; set aside to cool. Preheat oven to 325°F; flour and grease 10-inch bundt pan. Cream butter and sugar and add vanilla; alternately add eggs, flour (with baking powder and soda) and sour cream. Add ¼ cup Kahlúa to chocolate and coffee mixture and blend into other mixture; fold in nuts, pour into pan and bake for 1 hour and 30 minutes. Cool in pan 15 minutes. Invert on wire rack and sprinkle with remaining Kahlúa. May be topped with chocolate glaze. Yield: 12-14 servings.

GLAZE:
2 Tbsp. butter, melted
¼ c. powdered sugar

2 Tbsp. cocoa
Milk or cream

Combine butter and cocoa; add powdered sugar and mix well. Gradually add milk or cream, 1 tablespoon at a time until spreading consistency. Drizzle on top of cake, allowing some to run down the sides.

SNOWY WHITE FROSTING

1 c. sugar
½ c. water
1 tsp. vanilla

1 tsp. cream of tartar
2 egg whites

Combine sugar, water, cream of tartar in 2-cup Pyrex measure. Microwave 4 to 5 minutes on HIGH or until mixture boils (about 200°F). Beat 2 egg whites in small mixer bowl until soft peaks form. Gradually pour in hot syrup; beat about 5 minutes or until thick and fluffy. Blend in vanilla.

ITALIAN CREAM CAKE

5 large eggs
½ c. butter
½ c. shortening
1 tsp. baking soda
½ c. coconut
Cream Cheese Icing
(Recipe follows)

1 c. chopped nuts
1 tsp. vanilla extract
2 c. granulated sugar
1 c. buttermilk
2 c. all-purpose flour, sifted 2 times

Separate eggs and beat whites until stiff; set aside. Cream butter, shortening and sugar; add egg yolks, one at a time, beating well after each addition. Dissolve soda in buttermilk; add alternately with flour; beat well; add coconut, nuts and extract. Fold in stiffly beaten egg whites. Pour into 3 greased and floured 9-inch cake pans, using 2 cups batter for each pan. Bake in 350°F oven for 25 minutes. Cool cake completely then frost. Yield: 16-20 servings.

CREAM CHEESE ICING:
½ c. butter
1 tsp. Almond extract

1 (8 oz.) pkg. cream cheese, softened
1 lb. box powdered sugar

Combine ingredients and beat well. Spread between layers and on top of cake. Refrigerate.

SYLLABUB

1 c. dry white wine
¼ c. sugar
¼ c. brandy

1 Tbsp. lemon juice
2 c. whipping cream

Combine wine, sugar, brandy and lemon juice. Let stand until sugar is dissolved. Add cream and whip until soft and fluffy. Spoon into stemmed dessert glasses. Garnish each with lemon peel twists. Yield: 4½ cups.

Delicious when frozen and served like ice cream.

NEIMAN MARCUS BARS

4 eggs	1 box yellow cake mix
1 stick butter	1 (8 oz.) pkg. cream cheese
1 box powdered sugar	1 tsp. vanilla

Preheat oven to 350°F. Spray 9x13 inch pan with Pam or equivalent. Mix cake mix, 2 eggs and butter; spread in bottom of pan. Beat cream cheese until fluffy; add eggs, vanilla and powdered sugar; beat 2 minutes; spread on top of cake mixture. Bake 40 minutes; cool; cut into bars approximately 2x2-inches. Yield: 2 dozen bars.

ICE CREAM FLOAT

Rocky Road Ice cream	Kahlùa or Praline Liqueur
Mocha	Cherries or fresh strawberries

In a large mug, fill with Rocky Road ice cream, pour over 1 tablespoon Kahlùa and ¼ cup Mocha; top with cherries or fresh strawberries.

Option:

Vanilla ice cream	Amaretto or Peach Schnapps
Half and half	Fresh peaches or berries

CHEESE CAKE - NO BAKE

2 tsp. vanilla	1 (9 in.) deep dish pie crust (baked)
⅓ c. sugar	1 c. blueberry or peach pie filling
1 c. sour cream	1 (8 oz.) pkg. cream cheese, softened
8 oz. Cool Whip	

Beat cream cheese until smooth; gradually beat in sugar, blend in sour cream and vanilla; fold in Cool Whip, blend in well. Spoon into crust and top with pie filling. Chill until set, about 4 hours.
Yield: 6-8 servings.

LEMON SQUARES

½ c. softened butter	1½ c. plus 3 Tbsp. un-sifted flour
1½ c. granulated sugar	½ c. confectioners' sugar
1 tsp. baking powder	⅓ c. lemon Juice
4 eggs	1 tsp. lemon zest
1 c. chopped pecans	Additional confectioners' sugar

Preheat oven to 350°F. In medium bowl combine flour, ½ cup confectioners sugar and softened butter; press into bottom of lightly greased 9x13 inch baking pan; press in chopped pecans; bake 15 minutes. Meanwhile in large bowl combine granulated sugar, remaining 3 Tbsp. flour, baking powder, eggs, and lemon juice; mix well. Pour over baked crust; bake 20-25 minutes or until lightly browned. Cool. Cut into squares; sprinkle with additional confectioners sugar. Store covered in refrigerator. Yield: 24 squares.

MISSISSIPPI MUD CAKE

2 c. sugar	1 Tbsp. Kahlua
4 eggs	¾ c. chopped pecans
⅓ c. cocoa	1 (10½ oz.) pkg. miniature
2 sticks butter	marshmallows
1½ c. self-rising flour	

ICING

¼ c. butter	1 box confectioners' sugar
⅓ c. evaporated milk	¾ c. chopped pecans
⅓ c. cocoa	2 Tbsp. Kahlua

Cream sugar, eggs, cocoa, butter and Kahlua. Add flour and nuts. Stir until smooth. Bake in 9x13x2 inch baking dish at 300°F for 40 minutes. Remove from oven and cover entire cake evenly with marshmallows. Return to oven and bake an additional 10 minutes. Prepare frosting by heating butter, milk and cocoa. Place sugar in bowl, pour butter mixture over sugar, add Kahlua and stir until smooth. Add nuts and spread on top of cake. Yield: 10-12 servings.

ENTRÉES

ROAST STANDING RIBS OF BEEF

Have butcher cut short ribs and remove chine bones for easier carving. Place beef in roasting pan, fat side up so that meat is resting on the ends of the ribs. Do not add water. If a meat thermometer is available, insert the thermometer so that the bulb of the thermometer rest in the center of the large muscle of the roast. Thermometer should not rest on bone or in fat; cover; roast in a slow oven (300°F) according to the following schedule:

Rare beef ....140°F or 28 minutes per pound
Medium beef ......160°F or 32 minutes per pound
Well done beef ...170°F or 37 minutes per pound

Remove meat from oven and from roaster. Serve sliced, hot or cold.

POT ROAST
(CROCK POT)

6 medium potatoes   Select 3-3½ lb. roast beef
6 large carrots   1 pkg. Lipton onion soup mix
Creole seasoning   1 can cream of mushroom soup
Mrs. Dash   ½ c. water
Lemon pepper

Season roast with Creole seasoning; put in crock pot; add onion soup, potatoes, carrots (seasoned with lemon pepper and Mrs. Dash), cream of mushroom soup and water. Start crock pot on medium-high for first 20-30 minutes, then reduce to low and cook for eight hours or until done. Yield: approximately 1 serving per ½ pound of roast.

Hint: Freeze left over gravy and use for a meat loaf.

MEAT LOAF

2 lbs. ground chuck	1 tsp. Creole seasoning
2 eggs	½ c. warm water
1½ c. bread crumbs	1¾ c. seasoned pasta sauce, divided
1 pkg. onion soup mix	½ medium onion, chopped

Mix all ingredients throughly, (including 1 cup pasta sauce); put into large casserole dish; spread remaining cup of pasta sauce over top; bake in preheated 350°F oven for 1 hour. Yield: 6-8 servings.

SPAGHETTI SAUCE WITH FEDELINI

2 lbs. ground chuck	28 oz. seasoned pasta sauce
1 Med. onion, chopped	1 tsp. Creole seasoning
½ c. celery, chopped	1 pkg. Fedelini Angel Hair Pasta
½ c. green pepper, chopped	

In 5 quart Dutch oven, brown meat and sauté onion, celery and peppers together, chopping meat and turning continuously until meat is cooked; add pasta sauce and simmer for 45 minutes. Let sit on stove for approximately 1 hour and then reheat.

Cook 1 package of Angel Hair Fedelini (Venecia) according to directions and serve. Yield: 10-12 servings.

MARINATED CHUCK ROAST

3-4 lb. chuck roast
⅓ c. vinegar
Salt & pepper to taste

2 Tbsp. brown sugar
1 Tbsp. Worcestershire sauce
1 pkg. onion soup mix

Pierce roast with fork; mix ingredients for marinade; pour over roast and let stand 4 hours, or over night in refrigerator; turn roast occasionally.

Preheat oven to 300°F. Drain meat; wrap roast in heavy aluminum foil; place in baking pan and bake about 3 hours. Make gravy from drippings. Yield: 4-6 servings.

BEEF BRISKET

4-5 lb. beef brisket
1 c. water or beer
1 c. barbeque sauce
1 Tbsp. honey

1 tsp. Creole seasoning
1 pkg onion soup mix
⅓ c. oil & vinegar (Italian salad
   dressing)

Rub brisket with Creole seasoning; pour over vinegar and oil and marinate 3-4 hours; mix onion soup and water, pour over brisket (fat side on top); cover; cook at 275°F for 6 hours or longer; uncover last 2 hours; brush with mixture of barbeque sauce and honey last 20 minutes. Yield: 6-8 servings.

DAVE'S CAJUN GRILLED
EYE OF ROUND ROAST

1½ clove of garlic
Garlic powder
Black pepper
White pepper

2-2½ lb. eye of round roast
Creole seasoning
Meat seasoning

Insert garlic cloves into roast. Season heavy and roll seasoning into meat. Set aside for 1 hour or more. Place roast on hot side of grill and sear each side for 10 minutes. Put hickory chips on coals and move roast to cool side of grill; cook 20-25 minutes on each side or until done to taste. Yield: 4 servings.

PORK CHOPS & RICE

6-8 pork chops
2 Tbsp. vegetable oil
1½ c. uncooked rice
¼ c. chopped shallots
¼ c. chopped celery

½ tsp. salt
Creole seasoning
1 pkg. onion soup mix
1 c. water
¼ c. chopped green pepper

Preheat oven to 300°F. Brown chops in vegetable oil. In a large shallow baking dish, spread rice; add shallots, green pepper, celery, salt and Creole seasoning; top with chops. Mix soup with water and pour over chops; cover and bake for 1 hour. Yield: 6-8 servings.

PAN GRILLED PORK CHOPS

Worcestershire sauce
Season with salt and
  Creole seasoning

4-6 boneless pork chops
  (approximately ¾ inch thick)
½ c. water

Spray large non-stick skillet with Pam; season pork chops with salt and Creole seasoning; put in hot skillet and brown; meanwhile put a few drops of Worcestershire sauce on top of each pork chop; turn and repeat process; add approximately ½ cup water; cover and simmer for 10-12 minutes, turning once. Serve with long grain and wild rice. Yield: 4-6 servings.

COUNTRY STYLE BARBEQUE RIBS

3 lb. ribs
½ c. vegetable oil
1 c. water
2 tsp. salt
¼ c. cider vinegar
1 tsp. prepared mustard

1 pkg. onion soup mix
3 Tbsp. Worcestershire sauce
1 onion, finely chopped
½ c. finely chopped celery
1 c. barbeque sauce
1 Tbsp. honey, add to barbeque sauce

Mix all ingredients (except barbeque sauce and honey); pour over ribs and marinate overnight. Place in baking pan and bake at 275°F for 3-4 hours or until done. Uncover last 30 minutes and brush with barbeque sauce and honey. Yield: 4 servings.

PORK WITH WILD RICE & APPLES

1⅔ c. water	1 (6 oz.) pkg. Long Grain & Wild
⅔ apple juice	Rice Original Recipe
2 Tbsp. butter, divided	6 butterflied pork chops, well
1 tsp. ground coriander	trimmed, cut ½ inch thick
½ tsp. salt	(about 1½ lb.)
¼ c. apple jelly	1 c. chopped unpeeled red apple
¼ tsp. freshly ground	1 Tbsp. Dijon-style mustard
black pepper	⅓ c. toasted slivered almonds

Combine water, apple juice, 1 Tbsp. butter and contents of rice and seasoning package in medium saucepan; bring to a boil; reduce heat; cover and simmer until all liquid is absorbed, about 25 minutes. While rice simmers, sprinkle meat with combined coriander, salt and pepper; heat remaining 1 Tbsp. of butter in 12 inch skillet over medium heat; cook meat in skillet until no longer pink, about 4-5 minutes per side; remove and pour off fat if necessary. Add jelly and mustard to skillet; cook and stir until thickened and bubbly, about 2 minutes. Pour over meat. Stir apples and almonds into rice; serve alongside meat. Yield: 6 servings.

PORK TENDERLOIN

½ c. Italian Dressing
2 Tbsp. soy sauce
1 tsp Creole Seasoning

1½-2 lb. pork tenderloin
2 Tbsp. Worcestershire Sauce

Mix all ingredients, pour over pork and marinate for 4 hours; place in prepared baking bag and bake at 325°F for 35-40 minutes or cook on medium hot grill. Yield: 4 servings.

SAUSAGE-STUFFED ACORN SQUASH

¾ lb. pork sausage
½ c. sliced celery
½ c. onion, chopped
1 beaten egg
3 Tbsp. brown sugar

2 (1½ lb.) acorn squash, halved
  lengthwise and seeded
⅓ c. grated Parmesan cheese
1 small apple, chopped

Place squash, cut side down, in a large baking pan. Bake in a 350°F oven for about 45 minutes or until just tender.

Meanwhile, in a large skillet cook sausage, celery, and onion until meat is browned and vegetables are tender. Combine egg, cheese, brown sugar and apple; stir into sausage mixture. Turn squash halves cut side up; mound sausage mixture into squash shells. Cover and bake for 20-25 minutes more or until sausage mixture is heated through. Yield: 4 servings.

STUFFED ROAST TURKEY

1 c. minced onion	2 tsp. poultry seasoning
1 qt. diced celery	1 c. margarine or butter
1½ c. broth	1 tsp. salt
1 ready-to-cook turkey	½ tsp. pepper

4 qts. firmly packed bread cubes (2-4 days old)*
*May substitute corn bread

Cook onion and celery in butter or margarine until onion is soft but not brown; blend seasonings with bread; add onion & celery; toss ingredients together; pour broth over dressing, tossing ingredients lightly to blend well; adjust seasoning. Yield: 16 cups.
Allow 1 cup dressing per pound ready-to-cook weight of turkey.

Rub body cavity with salt; place dressing loosely in neck & body cavities of turkey; truss; place turkey in roasting pan, brush skin with melted butter/margarine and cover; roast in preheated oven at the designated temperature for various weights.

Approximate Ready-to-Cook Weight	Oven Temp.	Approximate Total Roasting Time - Hours
4 to 8 pounds	325°F	3½ to 4
8 to 12 pounds	325°F	4 to 4½
12 to 16 pounds	325°F	4½ to 5
16 to 20 pounds	300°F	5 to 6½
20 to 24 pounds	300°F	6½ to 8

When turkey tests done, remove it to a warm platter. Remove skewers and trussing cork. Prepare gravy with the pan drippings.

CHICKEN PARMESAN
(May substitute Veal)

½ lb. Provolone cheese slices
1 (1 lb.-10 oz.) jar pasta sauce

6 boneless chicken breasts, boiled and
chopped into bite sized pieces
½ bag fresh spinach leaves (frozen
can be used)

Put thin layer of sauce on the bottom of large baking dish and then layer as follows:

1. Spinach leaves
2. Chicken

3. Sauce
4. Cheese

Repeat layers a second time (so that cheese is on top). Cover and bake at 375°F about 35-40 minutes until it starts to bubble. Then remove cover and bake another 10-15 minutes until cheese starts to brown lightly.

BAKED CHICKEN BREAST

4 chicken breasts
2 can cream chicken
    mushroom soup
½ tsp. salt

¼ c. oleo
⅔ c. sour cream
¼ t. paprika
¼ tsp. pepper

Brown chicken in oleo; place in casserole; stir in seasoning and soup; cover and bake in preheated 350°F oven for approximately 45 minutes, or until tender; remove chicken, stir in sour cream and serve over noodles or rice.

ONE DISH CHICKEN & RICE

4 skinless, boneless	1 (10¾ oz.) can cream of mushroom
chicken breast halves	soup
1 c. water	¾ c. long-grain rice uncooked
¼ tsp. pepper	¼ tsp. paprika

In 2 qt. shallow baking dish, mix soup, water, rice, pepper & paprika; place chicken on rice mixture; sprinkle with additional paprika and pepper. Cover; bake at 375°F for 45 minutes or until done. Yield: 4 servings.

CHICKEN CASSEROLE

6 chicken breasts	½ soup can of milk
1 medium onion	1 can cream of mushroom soup
½ stick of butter	1 can cream of chicken soup
1 small pkg. cheddar cheese	1 (12 oz.) pkg. egg noodles

Salt, pepper and garlic to taste

Boil chicken breasts with salt, pepper and garlic. Debone and cut into chunks. Cook noodles in broth from chicken. Sauté onion in butter. Mix all ingredients in a casserole dish. Put cheddar cheese on top and bake in oven at 350°F for 30 minutes. Yield: 8 servings.

CHICKEN SAUCE PIQUANT

1 (3 lb.) chicken	2 (14½ oz.) can tomatoes
5 Tbsp. cooking oil	1 (8 oz.) can tomato paste
1 large onion chopped	1 clove garlic chopped
1 stalk celery chopped	¼ c. chopped bell pepper
3 Tbsp. flour	

Clean, debone & cut chicken into pieces; season to taste. Brown flour in oil; add onions, celery, bell pepper, & garlic; cook until tender; add tomatoes & sauce; stir well; simmer for approximately 45 minutes; add chicken pieces and cook slowly until chicken is very tender. Cover and let stand for 30 minutes to one hour. Reheat if desired; serve over white rice or spaghetti. Yield: 6 servings.

DUCK BREAST WITH TANGY HONEY SAUCE

¼ c. honey	4 duck breast halves (4-6 oz. ea.)
¼ c. soy sauce	½ c. canned crushed pineapple,
1 small clove garlic, minced	including syrup
½ tsp. ground ginger	¼ c. dry sherry or chicken broth
1½ tsp. cider vinegar	1 tsp. dry mustard
¼ c. Worcestershire sauce	1 Tbsp. orange juice concentrate
2 Tbsp. butter or margarine	Salt & pepper to taste

Combine pineapple, honey, sherry, soy sauce, vinegar, Worcestershire, orange juice, garlic, mustard & ginger in medium saucepan; bring to a simmer over medium heat; reduce heat to low; simmer 1 hour to blend flavors; strain and set aside.

Sprinkle breasts with salt & pepper to taste; arrange duck on rack in roasting pan; brush with butter; roast at 400°F for 40 minutes or until golden brown; then broil 3 to 5 minutes or until skin is crisp. Serve with sauce. Yield: 4 servings

CHICKEN WAIKIKI

1 chicken, cut up	1 tsp. salt
½ c. flour	¼ tsp. pepper
⅓ c. vegetable oil	

Season chicken with salt and pepper, coat with flour; heat oil in large skillet and brown chicken on all sides. Place chicken in a shallow roasting pan; arrange pieces, skin side up. Prepare sauce.

Sauce:

1 Tbsp. cornstarch	1 large can sliced pineapple
1 Tbsp. soy sauce	1 chicken bouillon cube
¼ tsp. ginger	1 c. sugar
¾ c. cider vinegar	1 large green pepper, sliced

Drain pineapple syrup into a 2 cup measure; add water to make 1¼ cups; mix cornstarch to dissolve. In medium saucepan, combine sugar, syrup with cornstarch, vinegar, soy sauce, ginger and bouillon cube; bring to a boil and cook for 2 minutes; pour over chicken; bake in 350°F preheated over for 30 minutes; add pineapple and pepper slices; bake 30 more minutes; serve with rice. Yield: 8 servings.

CHICKEN CACCIATORE

6 chicken thighs	1 (4 oz.) can mushrooms
¼ c. vegetable oil	1 (14½ oz.) can Italian tomatoes
½ c. dry wine	1 large onion, chopped
1 tsp. salt	1 (8 oz.) can tomato sauce
¼ tsp. pepper	1 or 2 bay leaves
¼ tsp. oregano	Romano cheese

Brown chicken in vegetable oil in large skillet; remove chicken from skillet; sautè onions, add remaining ingredients, except wine; blend well; add chicken to sauce; cover and simmer 45 minutes. Add wine; cook uncovered 20 minutes; remove bay leaves; serve over spaghetti; sprinkle with Romano cheese.
Yield: 6 servings.

MEXICAN CHICKEN

4 chicken breasts	1 pkg. corn tortillas
1 can evaporated milk	1 can cream of chicken soup
1 onion, finely chopped	1 can cream of mushroom soup
1 lb. grated cheddar cheese	1 can Ro-Tel tomatoes with green chiles

Boil chicken breasts; cut into large pieces; cut tortillas into 1 inch strips; mix soups, milk, onion and tomatoes; grease large baking dish; add 3 Tbsp. chicken broth; place tortillas on bottom; then add chicken; continue to layer. Marinate overnight in refrigerator; bake in 300°F oven for 1½ hours; sprinkle with grated cheese last 10 minutes of baking. Yield: 6 servings.

SOY HONEY CHICKEN

1-3 lb. fryer, cut	½ c. honey
into serving pieces	½ c. soy sauce
1 tsp. ground ginger	1 clove garlic, crushed
¼ c. dry sherry	

Combine honey, soy sauce, sherry, ginger and garlic in small bowl; place chicken in large Pyrex baking dish; pour honey marinade over chicken, turning chicken to coat; cover dish with plastic wrap; marinate in refrigerator at least 6 hours, turning 2 or 3 times.

Remove chicken from marinade, reserve marinade. Arrange chicken on rack over roasting pan; cover with foil; bake at 350°F for 30 minutes. Bring reserved marinade to a boil in a small saucepan over medium heat; boil 3 minutes and set aside.

Uncover chicken; brush with marinade; bake uncovered, 30 to 45 minutes longer or until juices run clear and chicken is no longer pink, brushing occasionally with marinade. Yield: 4 servings.

LEMON ASPARAGUS CHICKEN

4 skinless, boneless
chicken breast halves
1 can (10¾ oz.) cream
of asparagus soup
¼ c. milk
Lemon wedges

1 Tbsp. vegetable oil
1 Tbsp. lemon juice
⅛ tsp. pepper
½ tsp. salt
Hot cooked noodles
Fresh thyme

Season chicken with salt and pepper; brown in hot oil about 5 minutes per side; remove; set aside; spoon off fat. In skillet, combine soup, milk, lemon juice and pepper; heat to boiling; return chicken to skillet; cover; cook over low heat 5 minutes, or until chicken is tender, stirring occasionally. Serve over noodles. Garnish with lemon wedges and fresh thyme. Yield: 4 servings.

SKILLET CORN & CHICKEN

4 skinless, boneless
chicken breast halves
1 can (10¾ oz.) golden
corn soup
½ tsp. salt

1 Tbsp. butter
2 c. broccoli florets
⅛ tsp. pepper
½ c. shredded cheddar cheese

Season chicken with salt and pepper; brown in butter about 5 minutes per side; remove; set aside; spoon off fat. In skillet, combine remaining ingredients; heat to boiling; return chicken to skillet; cover; cook over low heat for 10 minutes or until chicken is tender and broccoli is tender-crisp, stirring often. Yield: 4 servings.

BARBEQUE CHICKEN

4 to 6 chicken breasts	Italian salad dressing
Salt and pepper	¼ c. honey

Wash and tear back skins, but do not remove; pat dry with paper towels. Season with salt and pepper; marinate in Italian dressing approximately 2 to 4 hours; baste chicken on both sides; peel skin out to cover chicken; place on rack of hot charcoal grill; turn to low setting. Turn chicken every 10 to 15 minutes basting each time; Grill for approximately 30 minutes. Add honey to remaining sauce and baste for last 15 minutes of cooking. Yield: 4 servings.

OVEN BAKED BARBEQUE CHICKEN

Preheat oven to 325°F, and follow above cooking directions. Roast for approximately 45 minutes.

BARBEQUE SAUCE

⅔ c. catsup	1 tsp. ground ginger
½ c. brown sugar	2 cloves garlic, minced
3 Tbsp. soy sauce	1 Tbsp. vinegar
1 tsp. Liquid Smoke	

Combine all ingredients in saucepan; heat until sugar is dissolved and mixture is bubbly. Yield: 1 cup.

ROCK CORNISH HENS

3 c. water	1 tsp. salt
1 c. wild rice	½ c. butter, melted
½ c. sliced, cooked mushrooms	6 Rock Cornish Game hens (thawed if frozen)
⅓ c. butter, melted	½ c. American Blue Cheese
3 tsp. salt	2 Tbsp. finely chopped onion

Bring water to boil; wash rice several times and add to boiling water with 1 tsp. salt. Cover and simmer for 1 hour without stirring until tender; drain if necessary; melt ½ cup butter; sauté onion and mushrooms in melted butter until lightly browned; toss lightly with wild rice and blue cheese.

Rinse hens with water and pat dry; rub cavities with salt; fill lightly with wild rice mixture. To close cavities, sew or skewer and lace with cord; tie legs together; brush with ⅓ cup melted butter. Roast uncovered at 350°F for 1 hour or until done. Yield: Serves 6.

ROCK CORNISH HENS
WITH WILD RICE STUFFING

3 Tbsp. butter
½ tsp. salt
1 c. water
1 tsp. lemon juice
2 Tbsp. chopped onion

2 (1 lb.) Rock Cornish Game hens
1 chicken bouillon cube
⅓ c. uncooked wild rice
½ c. chopped mushrooms, drained
Salt and pepper to taste

Season hens inside and out with salt and pepper. In small sauce pan, cook onion and rice in butter over medium heat for 5-10 minutes, stirring frequently; add water, bouillon cube, lemon juice, and salt; bring mixture to boiling, stirring to dissolve bouillon cube; reduce heat; cover and cook over low heat for about 20-25 minutes or until liquid is absorbed and rice is fluffy; stir in mushrooms; lightly stuff birds with the rice mixture.

Place birds breast up on rack in shallow baking pan; brush with melted butter or margarine tie drumsticks together loosely, if desired; close cavities with small skewers; lace with cord, if desired.

Roast uncovered at 350°F oven for 1 hour or until done. Yield: Serves 2.

BOILED SHRIMP/CRAB/CRAWFISH

Select fresh seafood and use crab and shrimp boil in concentrated liquid or bags. Follow directions for boiling; save the seasoned water and immediately use to boil small new potatoes or corn on the cob.

OYSTERS BIENVILLE

1 c. shrimp, chopped	2 doz. oysters on half shell
2 Tbsp. flour	1 No. 1 can mushrooms, chopped
2 Tbsp. butter	2 bunches shallots, chopped
1 c. chicken broth	½ c. Pernod or white wine
2 egg yolks	2 clove garlic, minced (optional)
Ice cream salt	Grated cheese (Parmesan or
Bread crumbs	American)
Paprika	

Place ice cream salt in pie plates or layer cake pans. Place oysters on half shell on salt. Bake oysters 350°F oven until partially done--about 6-8 minutes.

SAUCE: Sauté shallots and garlic in butter until brown; add flour, and heat until brown. Add chicken broth, shrimp and mushrooms. Beat egg yolks with wine and slowly add to sauce, beating rapidly. Season to taste. Simmer 10-15 minutes, stirring constantly.

Pour sauce over each oyster; cover with bread crumbs, paprika and grated cheese mixed. Place in oven to brown, about 12 minutes.
Yield: Serves 4 at ½ dozen each.

OYSTERS ROCKEFELLER

6 ribs celery, chopped
Juice of 2 lemons
1 c. water
1 c. bread crumbs,
   toasted
3 oz. Pernod
Tabasco and cayenne
Salt & pepper to taste

4 doz. oysters and shells
1½ lb. melted butter
1 bunch parsley, chopped
4 garlic cloves, minced
2 pkg. frozen spinach, cooked
   and chopped
1 bunch green onions, chopped
2 Tbsp. Worcestershire sauce

In a saucepan bring water to vigorous boil; add all vegetables; cover and reduce heat to simmer; cook 10 minutes. In a large skillet melt butter; add cooked vegetables, lemon juice, Tabasco, Worcestershire, cayenne, bread crumbs, salt and pepper; sauté until slightly thickened, stirring constantly; remove from heat and allow to cool slightly and add Pernod, mixing well.

Place oysters in cleaned half shells in pans filled with rock salt; broil at low temperature until edges curl, about 5 minutes; remove and pour water from each shell; cover each oyster with Rockefeller sauce; put back under broiler and brown slightly.
Yield: Serves 4 at 1 dozen each.

GALATOIRE'S TROUT MEUNIERE AMANDINE

½ lb. butter
Juice of 1 lemon
Oil for frying
Salt and pepper
Flour

4 (6-8 oz.) fillets of speckled trout
4 oz. sliced, toasted almonds
½ Tbsp. chopped parsley
Milk

Dip salt and peppered fillets in milk, then roll in flour. Fry in hot oil in shallow pan until golden brown on both sides. In separate pan, melt and continuously whip butter until brown and frothy. Add sliced almonds, lemon juice, parsley and pour over trout. Yield: 4 servings.

TROUT AMANDINE

6 fillets of trout
1 c. milk
1 tsp. salt
⅓ tsp. black pepper

½ c. sifted flour
¾ c. butter
½ c. sliced, toasted almonds

Dip fillets in milk, season with salt and pepper; roll in flour so entire fillet is well coated; melt butter in skillet and cook fillets, browning evenly on both sides; remove fish from skillet, add sliced almonds and sauté; sprinkle thickly over fish. Yield: 6 servings.

BAKED STUFFED FLOUNDER

½ lb. crab meat
2 Tbsp. chopped parsley
½ c. chopped celery
1 stick butter
1 clove garlic, minced
Salt, black pepper &
    cayenne to taste

½ c. chopped green onions
    (tops included)
1½ c. moistened bread cubes
½ lb. boiled shrimp, chopped
1 egg, slightly beaten
4 flounders, medium size

Saute celery, onion and garlic in ½ stick butter over low heat; add bread, shrimp, crab meat, parsley and egg; mix well; season with salt, black pepper and cayenne. Split thick side of flounder, lengthwise and crosswise, loosen meat from bone of fish to form a pocket for stuffing; brush well with melted butter; salt and pepper, and stuff pocket.

TO BAKE: Melt remaining ½ stick butter in shallow baking pan. Place fish in pan; do not overlap. Cover and bake in 375°F oven for 25 minutes, or until fish flakes very easily with a fork. Remove cover; bake another 5 minutes. Yield: 4 servings.

PICKLES, RELISHES AND JAMS

CRANBERRY RELISH

2 c. granulated sugar	1 lb. fresh cranberries
¼ c. fresh lime juice	¼ c. fresh orange juice
½ c. water	1 tsp. finely grated orange zest
1 tsp. finely grated lime zest	

Combine all the ingredients in a heavy saucepan. Bring to a boil, reduce heat to medium-low and simmer for 10 minutes or until berries pop open, skimming foam from the surface. Transfer to serving dish. Cool to room temperature. (The relish will set as it cools.) Yield: 8 servings.

PICKLED BEETS

½ c. sugar	3 #303 cans (or 6 c. beets)
1 c. vinegar	1 tsp. vanilla
2 Tbsp. cornstarch	1½ c. beet juice
24 whole cloves	3 Tbsp. cooking oil
3 Tbsp. catsup	dash salt
onions optional	

Mix all ingredients (except beets) in saucepan. Cook 3 minutes over medium heat, or until mixture thickens, add beets. Transfer to serving dish. Cool and refrigerate. Yield: 3 pints.

GREEN TOMATO PICKLES

5 qt. jars	25 large green tomatoes
10 Tbsp. dill seed	2½ tsp. cayenne pepper (hot)
2 tsp. pickling spice	10 garlic cloves
4 c. vinegar	4 c. water
5 whole cloves	5 tsp. salt

Wash, core and slice tomatoes and put into scalded jars; heat remaining ingredients to boiling; pour into jars; seal and process 20 minutes in boiling water. Let stand one month before using. Yield: 5 quarts.

CUCUMBER PICKLES

¼ c. pickling spices	7 lbs. or 2 gal. cucumbers
2 c. lime juice	4 lbs. sugar
4 qts. vinegar	8 to 10 quart jars
1 Tbsp. salt	

Soak cucumbers in 2 gallons water with the lime juice for 24 hours; drain and wash well and put in ice water for 3 hours; drain well. Combine sugar, vinegar, salt and pickling spices; pour over cucumbers and let set for 24 hours. Put on stove and cook for 1 hour or until crystalized and clear. Put in scalded jars and seal. Yield: 8-10 quarts

QUINCE BUTTER

6 large quince
1 c. brown sugar

1 c. sugar
Water as required below

Peel, core and chop quince into approximately ½ in. chunks; place in saucepan with 1 cup sugar and 1 cup water; cook on medium for 10 minutes stirring frequently; reduce heat to medium low, cook 15 minutes, stirring frequently; add ½ cup brown sugar and ¾ cup water; cook 15 minutes; add water as needed. Mash quince with potato masher until you have a consistency between sauce and pulp; add brown sugar as needed; simmer for another 15 minutes. Pour into scalded jars and seal, or cool and bag for freezing.
Yield: Approximately 3 pints.

MINCE MEAT

7 lbs. pears (cooking)
2 lbs. sugar
2 lbs. raisins
1 c. vinegar

2 tsp. cinnamon
1 tsp. allspice
1 tsp. cloves
1 lemon (juice and rind)

Grind all together and cook until thick. Put in scalded jars and seal while hot. Add pecans when you make pies. Yield: 12-15 pints.

SAUCE PIQUANTÉ

1 c. onions, chopped
1 qt. vinegar
1 tsp. cinnamon
½ c. brown sugar
2 tsp. ginger
1 tsp. cayenne pepper
1 tsp. nutmeg

1 gal. chopped ripe tomatoes
½ c. sweet green peppers, chopped
½ c. sweet red peppers, chopped
1 tsp. ground mustard
½ c. salt

Peel, core and chop tomatoes; chop onions and peppers fine; boil all ingredients, except the vinegar, together until soft and broken; add vinegar and simmer for 1 hour; stir frequently. Put in scalded jars and seal while hot. Yield: 8 pints

PEAR CHOW RELISH

2 qts. onions
12 cucumbers
2 jalapenos peppers
1 tsp. celery seed
4 Tbsp. dry mustard
3 Tbsp. turmeric
Salt as needed

4 qts. cooking pears, measured after
grinding
8 large sweet green peppers
4 c. sugar
8 Tbsp. sifted flour
Vinegar as needed

Peel pears, quarter, core and grind with cucumbers, peppers and onions; press out juice, salt to taste; sift flour, sugar, mustard, and turmeric together then add celery seed and mix with pears; cover with vinegar; boil until mixture thickens, approximately 15-20 minutes, stirring constantly. Put in scalded jars and seal. Yield: 8-10 pints.

PEACH JAM

2 Tbsp. lemon juice	2¼ c. fresh chopped or ground
1½ c. sugar	peaches
¾ c. water	1 box Sure-Jell fruit pectin

Combine fresh chopped peaches and lemon juice; throughly mix sugar into fruit and let stand for 10 minutes. Mix water and fruit pectin in a small saucepan; boil 1 minute, stirring constantly. Stir in the fruit, and continue stirring about 3 minutes. Ladle jam into 4 half pint scalded jars with screw tops, tighten and let stand at room temperature for 24 hours to set. Or use plastic containers, (for freezing), with snap lids and cover right away.
Yield: 4-half pints.

BREAD & BUTTER PICKLES

6 small onions	4 qts. cucumbers, sliced
2 Tbsp. salt	3 c. sugar
1½ tsp. turmeric	1½ tsp. celery seed
3 tsp. mustard seed	3 c. vinegar

Combine salt sugar, turmeric, celery seed, mustard seed and vinegar in sauce pan; bring to boil then add cucumbers and onion. Put in scalded jars and seal while hot. Process in canning pan; boil 15-20 minutes. Yield: 6-8 pints.

SWEET PICKLED FIGS

½ c. soda	3½ lbs. (9 pts.) figs
2 c. sugar	4 qts. water
½ c. water	1 c. red cider vinegar
1 Tbsp. cloves	3 sticks cinnamon
	1 Tbsp. allspice

Boil 4 quarts water in large sauce pan, add soda and drop in figs. Stir 1 to 2 minutes and pour off water. Rinse figs in 2 changes of water and allow to drain in colander. In large enamel or stainless steel saucepan, add sugar, ½ cup water, vinegar and spices; bring to boil; drop in figs and bring to rolling boil. At this point, turn off heat and cover saucepan immediately, set aside and let stand for 3-4 hours; repeat cooking process, until figs are syrupy and just beginning to lose firmness; remove from heat and fill scalded jars and seal Yield: 6-8 pints.

SWEET ZUCCHINI RELISH

10 c. grated zucchini	4 c. chopped onion
2¼ c. white vinegar,	2 Tbsp. salt
1 Tbsp. celery seed	3 c. sugar
1 Tbsp. pepper	1 Tbsp. ground turmeric

Combine zucchini, onion and salt in a large bowl, cover and refrigerate 8 hours or over night.

Transfer zucchini to a colander; rinse under cold running water; drain well and press between layers of paper towels.

Combine zucchini mixture, sugar and remaining ingredients in a Dutch oven; bring to a boil over a medium high heat; reduce heat to medium and simmer for 30 minutes, stirring often.

Pack hot mixture into hot jars, filling to ½ inch from top; remove air bubbles; wipe jar rims; cover and seal.

Process in boiling water for 15 minutes. Yield: 9 half pints.

CUCUMBER RELISH

2 qts. shredded
  cucumbers
2 c. onion, shredded
4 Tbsp. salt
4-6 jalapenos peppers,
  finely diced

1½ tsp. turmeric
2 tsp. celery salt
5 c. sugar
3½ c. vinegar
3 tsp. cinnamon

Mix first 4 ingredients, refrigerate 2-4 hours, drain well, press out excess moisture. Add sugar, turmeric, cinnamon, celery salt, and vinegar. Cook for approximately 45 minutes; ladle into sterilized jars, remove air bubbles; leave ¼ inch space at top of jars, wipe rim, seal, cool, and store in cool, dark, dry place. Yield 8 pints.

CHOW-CHOW RELISH

1½ c. chopped cabbage
1½ c. onions
1½ c. diced green beans
1½ c. sugar
2 Tbsp. celery seed
3 Tbsp. salt
1 tsp. mustard seed
3 c. white vinegar

2 c. chopped cucumbers
1½ c. chopped sweet red peppers
1½ c. chopped green tomatoes
1½ c. diced carrots
2 tsp. dry mustard
1 tsp. ground turmeric

Combine vegetables, sprinkle with salt; refrigerate 4-6 hours; rinse well and press out excess moisture. Combine vinegar, mustard, sugar, mustard seed, celery seed and turmeric in large sauce pan; simmer 10 minutes; add vegetable mixture and simmer 15 minutes; bring to boil. Pack boiling hot into sterilized jars, leaving ½ inch head space; remove air bubbles by sliding a rubber spatula between glass and food; wipe jar rims; center snap lid on jar; apply screw band until just fingertip tight. Place glass jars in canner and process for ten minutes in boiling water. Remove jars, cool and store in a cool, dark place. Yield: 4 pints.

PIES

PIE CRUST

1 c. flour (plain)	½ c. butter
3 Tbsp. milk	½ tsp. salt

Cream butter; add milk, flour and salt; roll out. Yield: 1 pie crust.

PECAN PIE

5 whole eggs	1¾ c. light Karo syrup
¾ c. sugar	2 c. pecans (broken & whole)
4 Tbsp. melted butter	2 tsp. vanilla
3 Tbsp. flour	2 unbaked 9" pie shells

Preheat over to 425°F. Mix flour & sugar, set aside; beat eggs, blend in melted butter, sugar & flour, syrup, vanilla. Sprinkle nuts over bottom of unbaked pie shells; pour syrup mixture over them and bake in hot oven at 425°F for 10 minutes, then reduce heat to 325°F and bake approximately 30 to 35 minutes longer.

Hint: Mold heavy duty foil into empty pie plate, take out and put foil under pie, trim foil to extend 2 inches beyond pie; lightly turn foil back over edge of pie to prevent edges from getting too brown and keeps pie from leaking into oven. Yield: 8 servings.

APPLE PAN DOWDY

1 stick butter	8 oz. evaporated milk
⅔ c. sugar	6 med. large apples, sliced
2¼ c. flour	(about 8 cups)
2 eggs	½ c. raisins
2 tsp. baking powder	½ c. pecans
2 tsp. cinnamon	½ c. brown sugar
	½ c. Amaretto, divided

Soak raisins in ⅓ cup Amaretto; cream butter & sugar, add eggs and mix; add flour and baking powder alternately with milk; add remaining Amaretto, set aside. Spread apples in greased 13x9x2 inch casserole, add raisins, pecans, and sprinkle with cinnamon and brown sugar; pour batter over apple ingredients. Bake at 350°F for 40 minutes, or until golden. Cool and serve. Yield: 10-12 servings.

PEACH COBBLER

⅔ c. sugar	3 c. sliced, peeled peaches
1 Tbsp. cornstarch	1½ tsp. butter
1 c. boiling water	½ tsp. cinnamon
1 recipe Pie Crust	

Mix sugar and cornstarch; stir in water; bring to boil and continue cooking 1 minute; add fruit. Pour into 10x6x2 inch baking dish; dot with butter; sprinkle with cinnamon. Top fruit with pie crust. Bake in 400°F oven for 30 minutes. Yield: 6-8 servings.

SHOO-FLY PIE

1½ c. flour
½ c. brown sugar
4 Tbsp. butter
½ c. dark corn syrup

½ c. hot water
½ tsp. baking soda, divided
1 tsp. cinnamon
1 (8 inch) unbaked pie shell

Mix flour, sugar and ¼ tsp. baking soda; cut in butter until crumbly; set aside. Combine corn syrup, ¼ tsp. baking soda and hot water; pour ½ mixture into pie shell; sprinkle with ½ flour mixture and repeat layering. Sprinkle with cinnamon; bake at 375°F for approximately 40 minutes. Cool and serve. Yield: 6-8 servings.

SWEET POTATO PIE

4 c. sweet potatoes
  baked and mashed
⅓ c. coconut
½ c. evaporated milk
Cool Whip

2 Tbsp. Amaretto
⅓ c. granulated sugar
⅓ c. brown sugar
½ stick butter, softened
¾ c. pecans (optional)

Cool, peel, chop/mash 3 large baked sweet potatoes in electric mixer bowl and mix with butter, sugar, milk and Amaretto; fold in coconut and pecans; bake in greased 9 inch pie plate at 350°F for approximately 35 minutes, or until beginning to brown around edge. Cool. Top with Cool Whip before serving. Yield: 8 servings.

Hint: Freezes well.

4 - LAYER DELIGHT

1 c. flour	½ c. chopped nuts
2 Tbsp. sugar	1 stick butter

Combine flour, sugar, nuts and butter; mix well; press in 9x13 inch Pyrex dish. Bake at 375°F for 15-20 minutes. Cool.

8 oz. cream cheese	1 c. powdered sugar
1 c. whipped cream	

Combine cream cheese, powdered sugar and whipped cream; spread over crust and refrigerate 15 minutes.

Instant pudding any flavor, (2 large)

Prepare instant pudding as directed; spread over cream cheese mixture and refrigerate 15 minutes.

Top with whipped cream and sprinkle with nuts. Yield: 16 servings.

(Wonderful for chocolate pie or for berry pie with vanilla pudding)

EGG CUSTARD

¾ c. sugar
2 Tbsp. flour
½ stick butter

4 eggs, lightly beaten
2 c. milk, scalded
2 tsp. vanilla

Mix flour and sugar; add milk, eggs and vanilla. Melt butter and pour in bottom of 1½ qt. casserole; pour in other ingredients; place casserole in large baking pan of hot water. Bake at 350°F for 45-50 minutes. Yield: 6 servings.

FROSTY AMBROSIA PIE

2 Tbsp. sugar
½ c. milk
*6 drops yellow food coloring
*3 drops red food coloring
1⅓ c. coconut
* Optional

1 (3 oz) pkg. cream cheese, softened
¼ orange with peel, seeds removed
1 (8 in.) graham cracker crust, prepared
1 c. whipped cream

Combine cream cheese, sugar, milk, food coloring, orange and coconut in blender. Cover and blend for 30 seconds. Fold into whipped cream. Spoon into crust. Freeze until firm, about 4 hours. Let stand at room temperature for 5 minutes before cutting. Garnish with orange slices. Store any leftover pie in freezer. Yield: 6-8 servings.

DUTCH APPLE PIE

1 egg white, beaten	1 graham cracker pie crust
1 Tbsp. lemon juice	5½ c. fresh, peeled, sliced cooking
½ tsp. ground cinnamon	apples
¼ tsp. nutmeg	¼ c. packed brown sugar
½ c. granulated sugar	3 Tbsp. all-purpose flour

Brush bottom and sides of pie crust evenly with egg white; bake on baking sheet at 375°F until light brown, about 5 minutes; remove crust from oven. In a bowl, combine apples, lemon juice, sugars, flour, cinnamon, and nutmeg; mix well; spoon into crust; sprinkle topping evenly over apples. Bake on baking sheet 50 minutes or until topping is golden and filling is bubbling. Cool. Yield: 6-8 servings.

TOPPING:

¼ c. granulated sugar	¾ c. all-purpose flour
⅓ c. butter	¼ c. packed brown sugar

In a bowl, combine flour and sugars; cut in butter until crumbly.

CRANBERRY PECAN PIE

½ c. orange juice
½ c. honey
2 Tbsp. cornstarch
2 Tbsp. cold water
½ tsp. orange extract

2 c. cranberries, (fresh or frozen)
1 baked 9-inch pie shell with
fluted rim
Pecan Topping (see below)

Combine cranberries, juice and honey in medium saucepan; cover; cook over low heat for 15 minutes (fresh) or for 20 minutes (frozen); cool; puree cranberry mixture in blender; return to saucepan; combine cornstarch and water in cup; stir into cranberry mixture; bring mixture to a boil over high heat and cook until thickened; stir in orange extract; cool, then pour into pie shell.

Spoon Pecan topping evenly over cranberry mixture. Bake in preheated 350°F oven for 20 minutes or until top is bubbly. Cool on wire rack. Serve at room temperature or chilled. Yield: 8 servings.

PECAN TOPPING:
½ c. honey
3 Tbsp. butter

1¾ c. pecan halves

Combine honey and butter in medium saucepan. Cook and stir over medium heat 2 minutes or until mixture is smooth. Add pecan halves and stir until well coated.

CREAMY LEMON PIE

3 egg yolks
1 (14 oz.) can sweetened
  condensed milk
Yellow food coloring,
  (optional)

1 (8 or 9-inch) baked pastry shell or
  graham cracker crust
½ c. ReaLemon Lemon Juice from
  concentrate
Whipping cream or Cool Whip

Preheat oven to 325°F. In medium bowl, beat egg yolks; stir in sweetened condensed milk, lemon juice and food coloring if desired. Pour into prepared pastry shell; bake 30 minutes; cool; spread with whipped cream; garnish as desired. Refrigerate. Yield: 6-8 servings.

Key Lime Pie: Substitute ½ cup Realime Lime Juice from Concentrate for Realemon and proceed as above.

COCONUT PIE

1 stick butter
3 Tbsp. flour
¾ c. sugar
1 tsp. vanilla

3 eggs, separated
½ c. milk
¾ c. flaked coconut, divided
1 (9-inch) baked pie shell

In heavy saucepan, melt butter over low heat; stir in mixed sugar and flour, egg yolks and milk, blending well; cook slowly until thickened. Add vanilla and fold in ½ cup coconut; cool to lukewarm. Pour into baked pie shell; top with meringue made from 3 egg whites and sprinkle remaining ¼ cup coconut on top. Bake at 325°F for 20 minutes or until golden brown. Cool. Yield: 8 servings.

CHOCOLATE NUT PIE

1 (9-inch) pie shell
3 eggs lightly beaten
½ c. light corn syrup
2 Tbsp. melted butter
1 tsp. vanilla extract

1 c. (16 oz.) pkg. semi-sweet
  chocolate morsels
2 c. assorted unsalted nuts
  (cashews, pecans, peanuts,
  macadamias, etc.)
½ c. light brown sugar, firmly packed

Sprinkle chocolate morsels over bottom of unbaked pie shell; top with nuts. Lightly whisk eggs with light brown sugar, corn syrup, butter and vanilla. Pour mixture slowly over the nuts, position nuts as desired. Bake in preheated 375°F oven for 40-50 minutes or until golden. Cool at least 30 minutes before slicing. Yield: 6-8 servings.

BANANA CREAM PIE

3 medium bananas
3 Tbsp. cornstarch
1⅔ c. water
3 egg yolks, beaten
2 Tbsp. butter
1 tsp. vanilla extract

1 (9-inch) baked pie shell
1 (14 oz.) can sweetened condensed
  milk
Whipped cream
ReaLemon Lemon Juice from
  Concentrate or Amaretto

In heavy saucepan dissolve cornstarch in water; stir in condensed milk and egg yolks; cook and stir until thickened and bubbly; remove from heat; add butter and vanilla; cool slightly. Slice 2 bananas; drizzle with Amaretto or lemon juice; arrange on bottom of pastry shell; pour filling over bananas; cover. Chill 4 hours or until set. Spread top with whipped cream. Slice remaining bananas; drizzle with Amaretto or lemon juice and garnish top of pie. Refrigerate. Yield: 6-8 servings.

LEMON CREAM PIE

½ c. lemon juice
1 can condensed milk
8 inch graham cracker crust

2 Tbsp. confectioners sugar
8 oz. whipped cream, divided
Grated rinds of 2 lemons, divided

Blend together milk, lemon juice and grated lemon rind; fold in ⅓ to ½
whipped cream and pour into pie shell; blend powdered sugar into
remaining whipped cream, top and sprinkle with remaining rind.
Yield: 6 servings.

CHERRY COBBLER

2 sticks butter
4 eggs
1 tsp. almond extract
2 tsp. baking powder
Powdered sugar (optional)

2 c. all-purpose flour
1 (21 oz.) can cherry pie filling
1½ c. granulated sugar
Whipped cream slightly sweetened

In large mixing bowl, cream together butter and sugar; add eggs; beat
until light and fluffy; add almond extract; stir in flour and baking
powder; mix until smooth. Butter a 13x9-inch cake pan; turn mixture
into pan; spoon the pie filling into the flour mixture and distribute
evenly. Bake at 350°F for 45 minutes or until done. Filling will sink
into cake while baking. To serve cut into 16 pieces; dust with
powdered sugar; spoon whipped cream over each serving. Great if
served warm. Yield: 16 servings.

Option:
Substitute blueberry pie filling.

SALADS
&
DRESSINGS

SPINACH SALAD

2 bags fresh spinach	2 (8 oz.) cans water chestnut, sliced
½ lb. fresh bean sprouts	

Wash and stem spinach; break into bite size pieces and drain; drain and rinse bean sprouts and water chestnuts; combine with spinach. Prepare dressing.

DRESSING:

2 tsp. salt	1 medium red onion, diced
⅓ c. catsup	¼ c. cider vinegar
¾ c. sugar	1 tsp. Worcestershire sauce
1 c. salad oil	

TOPPINGS:

½ lb. bacon	4 eggs, hard cooked

Blend dressing ingredients in blender and slowly add 1 cup salad oil; top salad with the 4 boiled eggs sliced in half and the ½ lb. bacon fried crisp and crumbled. Pour dressing over salad. Yield: 8 servings.

FAIRMONT SPINACH SALAD

1 pkg. fresh spinach	5 strips bacon
2 Tbsp. olive oil	2 Tbsp. red wine vinegar
3 Tbsp. Worcestershire	1 tsp. Dijon mustard
2 tsp. sugar	Black pepper to taste
	1 tsp. herb mixture (rosemary, tarragon & oregano)

Wash and dry spinach; remove stems; place in bowl. Cut bacon into 1-inch pieces; brown in skillet; drain; add herb mixture; mix well. Add oil, vinegar, Worcestershire, mustard & sugar and mix well; heat, add pepper; pour half of the hot dressing over salad; cover pan and let steam for approximately 15 seconds. Toss salad; serve, and pour remaining dressing with bacon over salad. Yield: 4 servings.

THREE BEAN SALAD

1 can green beans	1 onion sliced into rings
1 can yellow beans	½ chopped green pepper
½ c. vinegar	1 can red kidney beans
½ tsp. pepper	½ small jar chopped pimento
¼ c. sugar	½ c. salad oil
1 tsp. salt	

Drain beans and add green peppers, onion rings and cut pimentos. Combine sugar, vinegar, salt, pepper and salad oil. Pour over vegetables. Refrigerate. Yield: 6 to 8 servings.

LEMON-MARINATED VEGETABLES

1 c. lemon juice	1½ c. pure vegetable oil
4 tsp. salt	¼ tsp. hot-pepper sauce
1 tsp. sugar	1 clove garlic, mashed
1 tsp. chopped parsley	1 lb. small zucchini, sliced
1 large cauliflower head	2 (14 oz.) cans artichokes, drained
separated into florets	and halved

Combine oil, lemon juice, parsley, salt, sugar, garlic and hot-pepper sauce in large screw top jar. Place vegetables in separate bowl. Shake oil mixture well. Pour over vegetables. Cover. Marinate overnight. Drain vegetables. Arrange in bowl. Yield: 12 servings.

MARINATED CARROTS

¼ c. vinegar
½ c. sugar
1 can tomato soup
1 tsp. mustard
1 tsp. pepper
1 tsp. salt

5 c. cooked sliced carrots
1 sliced medium green pepper
1 tsp. Worcestershire sauce
½ c. vegetable oil
1 sliced medium onion

Cook carrots until done but firm; drain and cool. Mix other ingredients; add carrots; cover and marinate at least 12 hours. Yield: 10 servings.

FRUIT SALAD

1 (1 lb.) pkg. frozen
  strawberries
4-6 bananas

1 (20 oz.) can peach pie filling
1 (20 oz.) can mandarin oranges
1 (20 oz.) can pineapple chunks

Mix together; serve. Yield: 10 to 12 servings.

COLORFUL VEGETABLE MOLD

2 c. diced carrots
½ tsp. salt
1 medium cucumber
½ c. vinegar

1 (17 oz.) can green peas
1 (6 oz.) pkg. lime Jell-O
1 c. cheddar cheese cubes
Lettuce & mayonnaise

Drain carrots and peas, reserving liquid. Add enough water to liquid to make 3½ c.; heat; dissolve gelatin in hot liquid; add vinegar and salt. Chill until partially set; stir in carrots, peas, cucumbers and cheese. Pour into 2 qt. mold and chill until firm. Remove from mold; garnish with salad greens and dot with mayonnaise. Yield: 8 servings.

SEVEN LAYER SALAD

1½ c. mayonnaise
2 c. grated Swiss cheese
6 hard boiled eggs, sliced
½ c. chopped green onions
Salt & pepper to taste

2-3 c. fresh chopped spinach
1 lb. crisp bacon, crumbled
2-3 c. lettuce, chopped small
1 (8 oz.) can sliced water chestnuts
1 (10 oz.) pkg. frozen green peas
(uncooked, but thawed)

Spread mayonnaise on top of each layer; sprinkle with cheese.
Yield: 8 servings.

POPPY SEED DRESSING

½ c. salad oil
3 Tbsp. lemon juice
1 tsp. dry mustard

½ c. honey
2 tsp. poppy seed

Whisk together all ingredients in small bowl until blended. Cover and refrigerate. Yield: 1½ cups.

Hint: This dressing is delicious with green salads or fruit salads.

POTATO SALMON SALAD

2 tsp. olive oil
Lettuce (optional)
Cherry tomatoes
4 hard cooked eggs, halved
1 c. thinly sliced red bell
  pepper

6 Medium russet potatoes, cooked
  and cubed
1 lb. fresh or thawed salmon steaks,
  1 inch thick, or 1 (15½ oz.) can
  salmon)
1 (13½ oz.) can pitted ripe olives,
  drained

DRESSING:

6 Tbsp. olive oil
1 Tbsp. Dijon mustard

3 Tbsp. red wine vinegar
¼ c. chopped parsley
Salt and pepper to taste

Brush salmon with oil and broil 8-9 minutes, turning once, let stand 2
minutes, drain; or (for canned salmon) remove skin and bones and
break into chunks. Combine salad ingredients, line large bowl with
lettuce and place salad over lettuce, arrange tomatoes around the
edge of bowl; whisk together dressing ingredients and pour over
salad. Yield: 4-6 servings.

HOT GERMAN POTATO SALAD

10 medium potatoes
3 strips bacon
2 stalks celery, diced
1 medium onion, diced
1 dash pepper

flour (as needed)
¼ c. vinegar, hot
⅓ c. stock, hot
1 tsp. parsley, chopped

Cook potatoes in jackets; retain stock; peel and dice or slice potatoes while still hot. Fry bacon, remove; sauté celery & onions until clear; add enough flour to pick up excess grease; cook for 2 to 3 minutes; crumble bacon & return to skillet. Add hot vinegar & stock gradually, stirring until smooth and thickened; consistency should be like heavy cream. Adjust if necessary; add pepper; combine with potatoes and let stand for ½ hour before serving. Sprinkle with chopped parsley. May be served hot or cold. Yield: 12 servings.

CRANBERRY SALAD

1 pkg. lemon Jell-O
1 pkg. raspberry Jell-O
½ c. sugar
2 c. hot water

1 lb. raw cranberries, ground
3 oranges, finely chopped
1 lg. can crushed pineapple
1 c. chopped pecans

Dissolve Jell-O in hot water; add other ingredients & chill until firm. Hint: freeze cranberries before grinding. Yield 10-12 servings.

BRIDGE CLUB CHICKEN SALAD

1 tsp. black pepper	4 c. cooked rice (use while warm)
½ tsp. Creole seasoning	½ c. stuffed green olives, drained and
4 celery ribs, sliced	sliced
¼ c. sliced pimento	4 c. cubed and cooked chicken breasts
8 green onions, sliced	1 (15 oz.) can water chestnuts, drained
1 green pepper, diced	and sliced
½ c. mayonnaise	2 (6½ oz.) jars marinated artichoke
½ c. Ranch dip	hearts, coarsely chopped
1 Tbsp. lemon juice	1 Tbsp. Balsamic vinegar, (optional)

Combine all ingredients, including the artichoke marinade, in a large
bowl and toss gently until well blended and season to taste. Serve
with cherry tomatoes or guacamole, chilled or at room temperature.
Yield: 12 cups.

PINEAPPLE BUTTERMILK SALAD

1 (20 oz.) can crushed	1 large pkg. orange Jell-O
pineapple	1 c. whipped cream
2 c. buttermilk	½ c. pecans (optional)

Bring pineapple and juices to a boil; set off stove; stir in Jell-O; cool
until it starts to gel; stir in buttermilk, mix well; fold in whipped cream;
spoon into 9x12" baking dish; refrigerate until congealed.
Yield: 12 servings.

AMBROSIA

1 (20 oz.) can pineapple
  chunks in juice
½ c. flaked coconut
¼ c. chopped almonds
1½ c. seedless grapes
  (or Maraschino Cherries)

1 (11 oz.) can mandarin orange
  segments
1 c. miniature marshmallows
1 banana, peeled, sliced
1 (8 oz.) carton vanilla yogurt

Drain pineapple and oranges; use juice as a beverage.
Combine pineapple, oranges, banana, grapes, marshmallows, coconut
and almonds; fold in yogurt. Chill. Yield: 4 to 6 servings.

FRESH FRUIT SALAD

8 oz. pineapple tidbits
1 c. blueberries
4 Tbsp. honey
1 Tbsp. Amaretto
½ c. pecans (optional)
4 bananas (optional)

3 medium apples, peeled, cored and
  chopped
2 c. cooked cranberries
½ c. strawberry preserves
⅓ c. celery, finely diced

Mix apples, strawberry preserves, celery, cranberries, blueberries,
pineapple, honey, Amaretto and pecans; top each serving with ½
sliced banana. Yield: 8 to 10 servings.

SANGRIA SALAD

1½ c. Rosé wine
¾ c. sugar
1 c. orange juice
2 Tbsp. lemon juice
3 oranges, peeled
Lettuce leaves

2 env. unflavored gelatin
1 large apple, cored & cut into
 chunks
1 c. red grapes, halved and seeded
4-5 drops red food coloring

In saucepan mix gelatin & sugar; stir in 1½ c. water; cook & stir until gelatin dissolves; remove from heat; stir in wine, orange juice, lemon juice & food coloring; chill until partially set (consistency of egg white). Fold in fruits; turn into a 6½ c. mold; chill until firm; unfold on a lettuce-lined platter; trim with frosted grapes if desired.
Yield: 8 to 10 servings

Frosted grapes: Break ½ lb. red grapes into small clusters; dip into 1 beaten egg white; drain; dip fruit into sugar to coat; dry on rack for 2 hours.

ITALIAN PASTA SALAD

2 c. uncooked pasta swirls
1 c. Italian Olive Salad
½ tsp. Bon Apetit seasoning

1 (5 oz.) can sliced water chestnuts
¼ c. grated Parmesan cheese
1 large can salmon with
 ½ tsp. lemon juice (optional)

Cook pasta swirls until done; drain and immediately return to hot pot; add Italian Olive Salad, Parmesan cheese and mix together well. Let sit for about an hour. Add water chestnuts and salmon.
Yield: 6 servings.

FRESH CRANBERRY SALAD

1 c. blueberries	3 c. fresh cranberries
3 medium tart apples	1½ c. sugar, divided
4 Tbsp. honey	8 oz. pineapple tidbits
1 Tbsp. Amaretto	½ c. pecans
8 oz. Cool Whip	4 bananas

Cook cranberries in ¾ c. sugar until syrupy; pop cranberries with slotted spoon or potato masher while cooking; cool; cook blueberries in ¼ c. sugar; peel & chop apples; add ½ c. sugar, honey, blueberries, pineapple, Amaretto and pecans; fold in cranberries; serve with banana & cool whip topping.
Yield: 10 to 12 servings.

MARINATED COLESLAW

2 medium white onions sliced	1 medium head of cabbage, shredded
½ c. sugar	

DRESSING:

1 tsp. celery seed	1 tsp. dry mustard
1 tsp. sugar	1 c. white vinegar
1½ tsp salt	1 c. salad oil

Stir ½ cup sugar into cabbage and place half in large bowl; cover with onion rings; cover with remaining cabbage. Combine dressing ingredients, except oil, in saucepan; bring to rolling boil; stir in oil and bring to boil again. Pour over cabbage and onions, do not stir. Refrigerate for 24 hours. Yield: 6-8 servings.

MARSHMALLOW-LIME SALAD

⅓ c. mayonnaise	1 (6 oz.) pkg. lime Jell-O
¾ c. hot water	1 (3 oz.) pkg. cream cheese
½ c. pecans	1 sm. can crushed pineapple
½ c. milk	14 large marshmallows

Dissolve Jell-O with hot water; add cream cheese and marshmallows; remove from stove; cool; add other ingredients, congeal in refrigerator. Yield: 12 servings.

CRANBERRY MOUSSE

2 c. whipped cream	2 c. fresh cooked cranberries
2 c. boiling water	1 (6 oz.) pkg. cherry Jell-O
½ c. pecans (optional)	1 (3 oz.) pkg. cream cheese,
¼ c. brown sugar	at room temperature
¼ c. granulated sugar	

Cook cranberries in brown sugar; pop cranberries with slotted spoon or potato masher while cooking, set aside; whip cream cheese until fluffy; fold into whipped cream; dissolve gelatin in large bowl with hot water; cool until mixture gets thick, but not firm; add cranberries and blend well; add cream cheese mixture and pecans and fold; place in a 6-cup mold or in individual molds; chill. Yield: 8 to 10 servings.

ORANGE-GLAZED BEETS

¼ c. honey
¼ c. orange juice
¼ c. lemon juice
½ tsp. salt

1 (1 lb.) can sliced beets, well drained
1 tsp. shredded orange peel

In small bowl, combine honey, orange peel, salt, orange & lemon juices; add drained beets; mix gently; refrigerate several hours; serve as relish. Yield: 6 to 8 servings.

MIXED-BERRY CHAMPAGNE AMBROSIA

¼ c. honey
2 Tbsp. lime juice
6 small sprigs mint
  for garnish

2½ c. fresh berries, mixed*
2 large sprigs fresh mint
2 c. chilled champagne or
  other sparkling white wine

*raspberries, blueberries, tiny strawberries, blackberries or pitted cherries

In a small saucepan, combine honey, lime juice and 2 large mint sprigs; warm over low heat just until the honey melts; remove from heat and let steep 5 minutes; discard mint, cool, place fruit in a large bowl, pour honey mixture over fruit and stir gently to combine. Divide berry mixture among 6 goblets or dessert dishes and refrigerate until ready to serve, up to 1 hour. Just before serving, pour the champagne over the fruit. Garnish each serving with a sprig of mint and serve. Yield: 6 servings.

GALATOIRE'S GODCHAUX SALAD

4 oz. Creole mustard	1 head iceberg lettuce, cubed
2 large tomatoes, cubed	1 lb. backfin lump crab meat
5 oz. salad oil	30-35 large shrimp, boiled, peeled
5 oz. red wine vinegar	and de-veined
2 hard cooked eggs	1 small can flat anchovies

In large salad bowl, combine lettuce, tomatoes, crab meat, and shrimp.

In small bowl, combine salad oil, red wine vinegar, and Creole mustard; mix well; pour over salad and toss. Divide salad onto 4 chilled plates and garnish each with ½ sieved hard boiled egg and 2 anchovies. Yield: Serves four as an entrée.

SHRIMP SALAD

2 c. cooked shrimp	1 c. celery coarsely chopped
¼ c. mayonnaise	½ tsp. Worcestershire sauce
1 Tbsp. catsup	2 hard-cooked eggs, coarsely
2 Tbsp. dill relish	chopped
3 tomatoes, sliced	Salt and pepper to taste

If shrimp are large, cut into halves or quarters. Mix shrimp, celery, eggs, and relish together lightly with mayonnaise, catsup, Worcestershire sauce, salt and pepper. Serve on lettuce leaves and garnish with sliced tomatoes. Yield: 4 servings.

CRANBERRY FRUIT MOLD

1½ c. cold ginger ale, lemon-lime carbonated beverage or water*

1 8 oz. pkg. cranberry Jell-O
2 c. halved green and/or red seedless grapes
1 11 oz. can mandarin orange segments, drained

Stir boiling water into gelatin in large bowl at least 2 minutes until completely dissolved; stir in cold ginger ale; refrigerate about 1½ hours or until thickened. Stir in fruit; spoon into 6-cup mold; refrigerate 4 hours or until firm. To unmold; dip mold in warm water for about 15 second; gently pull gelatin from around edges with moist fingers; place moistened plate on top of mold; invert mold and plate together, shake slightly to loosen; gently remove mold and center gelatin on plate; garnish as desired. Yield: 10 servings.

HOT SAUCE DRESSING

½ c. cider vinegar
⅓ c. sugar
2 Tbsp. olive oil
1 tsp. Tabasco sauce
½ tsp. celery seed

1 clove garlic, minced
1 tsp. Creole seasoning
2 Tbsp. Dijon mustard
2 Tbsp. pickled jalapeño juice

Combine all ingredients; mix well and refrigerate. Use as slaw or salad dressing.

Option: Mix with Ranch dip to desired consistency; use as salad/slaw dressing, in vegetables/casseroles, in potato salad, or as a sandwich spread. Try it on your BLTs.

WINTER SALAD

½ c. chopped onions
½ c. chopped carrots
¼ c. bacon bits
1 c. grated cheese

1 head cauliflower (florets)
1 bunch broccoli (florets)
¼ c. chopped green onion

Combine all ingredients in large bowl and set aside.

DRESSING:
½ c. mayonnaise
1 Tbsp. sugar

⅓ c. vinegar
⅓ c. salad oil
Salt and pepper to taste

Combine all dressing ingredients, adding salt and pepper to taste.
Pour mixture over vegetables. Refrigerate 12-24 hours, stirring
3 or 4 times. Yield: 8 servings.

ITALIAN POTATO SALAD

6 med. large potatoes
⅓ c. chopped onion
½ c. chopped celery
¼ c. chopped cucumber
2 Tbsp. mayonnaise
½ tsp. prepared horseradish

⅓ c. Italian salad dressing
4 hard-cooked eggs, chopped
¼ c. chopped green pepper
½ c. sour cream
Chopped fresh tomatoes (optional)

Peel and cube cooked potatoes; place in large bowl; add dressing and
toss to coat; cover and chill for 2 hours; add eggs, celery, onion,
cucumber and green pepper; mix well. In small bowl, combine
mayonnaise, sour cream and horseradish; pour over potato mixture
and toss to coat. Chill at least 1 hour. Top with tomatoes (optional).
Yield: 8-10 servings.

HONEY MUSTARD DRESSING

¾ c. mayonnaise
⅓ c. vegetable oil
¼ c. honey
¼ c. lemon juice

1 Tbsp. prepared mustard
1 tsp. pepper
½ tsp. minced onion flakes
1 Tbsp. minced fresh parsley

Whisk together all ingredients in small bowl until smooth and creamy. Cover and refrigerate until ready to serve. Yield: 2½ cups.

Hint: This dressing is wonderful on tossed green salads, spinach or with chicken or seafood salads.

BROCCOLI & CAULIFLOWER SALAD

⅔ c. mayonnaise
2 Tbsp. sugar
⅓ c. vinegar

1 lb. cauliflower (florets)
1 lb. broccoli (florets)
onion, optional

Break cauliflower and broccoli into small florets; wash and drain throughly. Mix mayonnaise, sugar, vinegar into a sauce; pour over vegetables; marinate overnight, turning several times. Yield: 6-8 servings.

LeRUTH'S AVOCADO DRESSING

1½ c. mayonnaise
1 lemon, juice only
½ tsp. salt
1 tsp. anchovy paste

1 mashed ripe avocado
1 tsp, crushed black pepper
1 toe garlic, chopped
¼ c. whipping cream

Mix well and refrigerate. Yield: 3 cups.

FIESTA BEAN SALAD

2 c. cold cooked rice
¼ c. Italian dressing
½ tsp. salt
1 tsp. ground cumin
1 medium red bell pepper,
    chopped

1 16 oz. can kidney beans, rinsed and
    drained
1 can (about 8 oz.) whole kernel corn,
    drained
½ c. sliced green onions with tops
½ to ⅔ c. piquanté sauce, as desired

Combine rice, beans, corn, bell pepper and green onions in medium bowl. Combine piquanté sauce, dressing, cumin and salt; pour over rice mixture; toss; cover and chill. Yield: 6-8 servings.

TUNA SALAD
(Jazz' Favorite)

1 (12 oz.) can tuna
½ tsp. lemon juice
1 tsp. celery seed

½ tsp. Creole seasoning
½ c. sweet relish
4 boiled eggs, chopped

Drain tuna well, add lemon juice and break up tuna with a fork; add celery seed, Creole seasoning, sweet relish, and eggs; mix well (by hand); refrigerate. Yield: 6 servings.

WALDORF CHICKEN SALAD

¼ c. honey
2 Tbsp. Dijon mustard
1 Tbsp. poppy seeds
⅓ c. lemon juice
¼ c. vegetable oil
¼ c. green onions, minced
1 c. diced celery

2 c. cubed cooked chicken or turkey
2 apples cored and diced
⅓ c. sliced or diced almonds
½ tsp. grated lemon peel
12 dried apricots (moist pack
　 preferable)

Stir together honey, mustard, poppy seeds, lemon juice, lemon peel and oil in large bowl; add apricots and let stand 30 minutes. Add chicken and toss lightly. Refrigerate until ready to serve.

Before serving add apples, celery, almonds and green onions to chicken mixture; toss to coat. Yield: 6 servings.

ITALIAN OLIVE SALAD

½ c. celery, chopped
½ c. carrots, chopped
¼ c. capers
2 Tbsp. parsley
1 tsp. oregano
2 garlic cloves, minced
1 c. olive oil

½ c. black olives, partially chopped
½ c. stuffed olives, partially chopped
½ c. green olives, cracked
½ c. cauliflower, chopped
½ c. sweet red pepper, chopped
1 tsp. Creole seasoning

Mix ingredients, cover with olive oil and and leave un-refrigerated overnight. Yield: 1 quart.

Great for pasta salads, tossed green Italian salads and muffulettas.

SANDWICHES
&
SAUCES

PHILLY CHEESE STEAK SANDWICHES

1 Tbsp. flour	1 beef bouillon cube, crushed
¼ c. steak sauce	1 lb. beef sirloin steak, cut in thin
⅓ c. water	strips
4 sub sandwich rolls	1 medium green pepper, cut in strips
1 medium onion, thinly sliced	2 Tbsp. cooking oil
4 slices American cheese	Salt & pepper

Season steaks with salt and pepper; flour; brown in skillet; add onions and peppers, beef bouillion, steak sauce, and water; simmer covered 10-15 minutes; uncover and cook slowly until liquid is absorbed.

Divide beef pieces, onions and peppers evenly onto 4 sandwich rolls, add cheese slices, and serve. Yield: 4 sandwiches.

BACON, LETTUCE & TOMATO SANDWICH

On rye or pumpernickle spread ranch dip with hot sauce; place crisp bacon, lettuce and tomatoes and serve.

Note: Recipe for Ranch Dip with Hot Sauce is in the SANDWICHES & SAUCES Section under "HOT SAUCE".

NEW ORLEANS MUFFULETTAS

Italian buns or French bread

Thinly sliced:
Hard Genoa salami
Ham (Prosciutto optional)
Mortadella
Imported Swiss or Provolone cheese

Layer meats and cheese on bread, top with Italian Olive Salad, heat and serve.

ITALIAN OLIVE SALAD

½ c. celery, chopped	½ c. black olives, partially chopped
½ c. carrots, chopped	½ c. stuffed olives, partially chopped
¼ c. capers	½ c. green olives, cracked
2 Tbsp. parsley	½ c. cauliflower, chopped
1 tsp. oregano	½ c. sweet red pepper, chopped
2 garlic cloves, minced	1 tsp. Creole seasoning
1 c. olive oil	

Mix ingredients, cover with olive oil and and leave un-refrigerated overnight. Yield: 1 quart.

Great for pasta salads, tossed green Italian salads and muffulettas.

SAVORY SAUCE PIQUANTÉ

2 med. chopped onions	3 celery stalks, chopped
3 green onions, chopped	½ c. fresh parsley, finely chopped
½ large bell pepper, chopped	1 (15 oz.) can tomato sauce
2 cloves minced garlic	1 (10 oz.) can Ro-Tel tomatoes
2 whole bay leaves	1 (14½ oz.) can stewed tomatoes
½ tsp. thyme	1 Tbsp. Worcestershire Sauce
½ tsp. salt	½ lemon, grated peel and juice
½ tsp. pepper	½ c. chopped mushrooms, (optional
½ tsp. Tabasco	½ tsp. Creole seasoning

Make a roux (2 Tbsp. flour & 2 Tbsp. shortening browned); in a 5 quart Dutch oven; add onions, cook until transparent; add stewed tomatoes, Ro-Tel tomatoes and tomato sauce; bring to simmer; add rest of ingredients; simmer for 20 minutes. Use with Redfish Courtbouillion or Jambalaya; as a dip, or with other recipes, i.e., spaghetti sauce, etc. Yield: 5-6 pints.

HONEY MUSTARD SAUCE

½ c. honey	½ c. Dijon mustard
4 tsp. olive oil	4 Tbsp. white wine vinegar
Salt & pepper to taste	2 tsp. dried tarragon, crushed

Combine mustard and tarragon in medium bowl; mix well. Gradually blend in honey. Whisk in vinegar and oil, mixing well. Add salt and pepper to taste. Serve with turkey or pork. Yield: 1 cup.

HONEY SWEET & SOUR SAUCE

1 c. catsup
4 Tbsp. lemon juice
1 tsp. garlic salt

½ c. honey
1 tsp. corn starch
2 tsp. dried tarragon, crushed

Combine all ingredients; cook and stir over medium heat 2-3 minutes or until mixture boils and thickens. Cool. Serve with fish or chicken. Yield: 1 cup.

HOT SAUCE

½ c. cider vinegar
⅓ c. sugar
2 Tbsp. olive oil
1 tsp. Tabasco sauce
½ tsp. celery seed

1 clove garlic, minced
1 tsp. Creole seasoning
2 Tbsp. Dijon mustard
2 Tbsp. pickled jalapeño juice

Combine all ingredients; mix well and refrigerate. Use as slaw or salad dressing.

Option: Mix with Ranch dip to desired consistency; use as salad/slaw dressing, in vegetables/casseroles, potato salad or as a sandwich spread. Try it on your BLTs.

BASIC WHITE SAUCE

2 Tbsp. melted butter   2 Tbsp. all-purpose flour
¼ tsp. salt   1 c. milk

In a 1½-quart casserole, combine melted butter, flour and salt.
Gradually add milk; stir until smooth. Microwave at MEDIUM 5-7
minutes, until sauce is thickened, stirring every minute with wire
whisk.

CHEESE SAUCE: Stir in ½ to ¾ cup shredded cheese. Microwave at
MEDIUM 1 minute, if necessary, to completely melt cheese.

CURRY SAUCE: Stir in 1-2 teaspoons curry powder.

HORSERADISH SAUCE: Stir in 1 tablespoon prepared horseradish.

SPICY COCKTAIL SAUCE

2 cloves garlic, minced   ½ c. finely chopped onion
1 Tbsp. butter   1 (6 oz.) can tomato paste
1 Tbsp. lemon juice   2 Tbsp. prepared horseradish
⅛ tsp. salt   1 tsp. Worcestershire sauce
1¼ c. water   ⅛-¼ tsp. ground red pepper

In medium saucepan cook onion and garlic in butter until onion is
tender. Stir in water, tomato paste, horseradish, lemon juice,
Worcestershire sauce, ground red pepper and salt. Simmer, uncovered
about 10 minutes or until slightly thickened. Cover and chill for
several hours.

CREOLE SAUCE

¼ c. chopped green pepper
½ c. chopped onion
1 bay leaf
1 sprig thyme
2 Tbsp. butter
½ tsp. sugar

1 can (1 lb. 13 oz.) tomatoes
1 tsp. chili powder
2 stalks celery, chopped
1 clove garlic, minced
Salt and pepper to taste

Saute green pepper, onion, celery and garlic in butter. Add tomatoes and seasonings. Simmer for 40 minutes, stirring frequently.
Yield: 2½ cups.

This is a basic sauce used with many Creole dishes, such as baked fish, shrimp and vegetables.

REMOULADE SAUCE

1 clove garlic
1 c. salad oil
½ c. tarragon vinegar
½ c. chopped celery
1 Tbsp. paprika

4 Tbsp. horseradish mustard
½ c. chopped green onions
2 Tbsp. tomato catsup
½ tsp. cayenne
1 tsp. salt

Blend all ingredients thoroughly. Yield: 2 cups.

When used with boiled shrimp allow shrimp to marinate for about 4 hours before serving.

LEMON DILL YOGURT SAUCE

¼ c. extra-virgin olive oil
2 tsp. chopped fresh dill
1 Tbsp. fresh lemon juice

1 c. plain nonfat yogurt, drained
1 tsp. finely grated lemon zest
¼ tsp. coarsely ground black pepper

Combine the yogurt, lemon juice and zest in a small bowl. Slowly drizzle in the olive oil, whisking constantly until smooth and slightly thick. Fold in the black pepper and chopped dill. Yield: 1¼ cups.

Notes

SOUPS, GUMBOS & STEWS

CUCUMBER SOUP

¼ tsp. white pepper
1 Tbsp. white vinegar
Salt to taste
¾ c. sour cream
¼ tsp. dill

4-5 large cucumbers, peeled & scored
½ tsp. chicken bouillon granules
⅓ c. chopped green onions
Fresh or dried dill leaves
Handful of watercress

In blender briefly process cucumbers, green onions, vinegar, salt, watercress, dill, white pepper, and ½ cup sour cream. Taste and adjust seasoning. Refrigerate 1-2 hours.

Before serving adjust seasoning and stir in remaining sour cream. Garnish with cucumber slices and dill leaves. Yield: 6 servings.

AVOCADO SOUP

2 tsp. lemon juice
2 c. water
6 small sprigs of mint
½ tsp. hot pepper sauce

2 c. light sour cream
2 medium ripe avocados
2 chicken bouillon cubes

Peel avocados; remove pits and slice; put slices in blender with sour cream, lemon juice, hot pepper sauce and water; crumble bouillon cubes on top; blend. Pour into bowls and chill in refrigerator for two hours. Garnish with mint before serving. Yield: 6 servings.

CHICKEN & RICE SOUP

1 (3 lb.) fryer	¾ c. rice
8 c. water	1 Tbsp. lemon juice
2 Tbsp. salad oil	1 tsp. salt
½ tsp. thyme leaves	2 celery stalks, chopped
1 carrot grated	¼ tsp. black pepper
1 onion, chopped	3 cubes chicken bouillon
3 Tbsp. flour	

Cook chicken in water until fork tender; refrigerate; skim fat from broth; debone chicken and cut into small pieces. In 2 quart saucepan over medium heat, in hot oil, cook celery, carrots and onion until tender; add flour; cook 1 minute, stirring constantly; slowly add 1 cup of broth to vegetables and cook, stirring until mixture is thickened. To remaining chicken broth add rice, lemon juice, salt, thyme, pepper, bouillon and vegetables; heat to boiling; reduce heat to low; cover and simmer 20 minutes, stirring occasionally; combine with vegetable mixture and add chicken. Yield: 12 servings.

CREAMY BROCCOLI SOUP

2 c. milk	¾ lb. Velveeta cheese, cubed
¼ c. chopped onion	1 (8 oz.) pkg. cream cheese, cubed
¼ tsp. nutmeg	1 (10 oz.) pkg. frozen broccoli cooked &
1 Tbsp. butter	drained
Dash of pepper	

In 2 quart saucepan, cook onion in butter until tender; add milk and cream cheese; stir over medium heat until cream cheese is melted. Add remaining ingredients; heat throughly, stirring often. Yield: 4 servings.

GOLDEN CREAM OF POTATO SOUP

1 tsp. salt	6 c. red potatoes, peeled, cubed
2 tsp. parsley flakes	½ c. onion, finely chopped
⅛ tsp. pepper	¾ lb. processed cheese, cubed
3 c. milk, divided	1 c. carrots, thinly sliced
¼ c. flour	1 c. celery, sliced
2 c. water	2 cubes chicken bouillon

Combine all ingredients, (except milk, flour and cheese), in a Dutch oven; bring to boil; cover, reduce heat and simmer 7-8 minutes or until vegetables are tender. Gradually stir ¼ c. milk into flour making a smooth paste; stir into soup; add remaining milk and cheese; cook over medium heat until soup is thick. Yield: 9 cups.

POTATO SOUP

4 c. chicken broth	2 Tbsp. parsley
4 medium potatoes	½ c. sour cream
1 Tbsp. butter	3 yellow onions, chopped
½ tsp. salt	

Simmer broth and add salt. Cut potatoes into eighths; add potatoes and onions to broth; cover, simmer for 20 minutes; add parsley and sour cream; simmer 5 minutes; add butter. Yield: 6 servings.

CREAM SOUP

½ tsp. dried basil	1 c. non-fat dried milk powder
¼ tsp. black pepper	2 Tbsp. chicken bouillon granules
½ tsp. dried thyme	1 Tbsp. dried onion flakes
2 Tbsp. corn starch	

This is a dry mix that can be stored in an air-tight container and kept on hand until it's needed.

When you are ready for soup, just add 2 cups of cold water and cook over medium heat, stirring constantly until it thickens. If the soup is too thick, just add a little more water.

For cream of mushroom soup, add some sliced mushrooms a few minutes before serving.

ZESTY TORTILLA SOUP

½ c. green onions, chopped	1 (14 oz.) can whole tomatoes, chopped, undrained
1 c. diced onion	
2 Tbsp. oil	4 (8 inch) flour tortillas
Fresh cilantro	1 (14 oz.) can chicken broth
1 c. Monterrey jack cheese, shredded	2 cloves garlic, minced
	46 oz. can Spicy Hot V-8 Vegetable Juice

Heat oven to 375°F. Stack tortillas and cut into ½ inch wide strips; place in single layer on ungreased baking sheet; bake for 15 minutes or until crisp and toasted; set aside. Sauté onions and garlic in oil in stock pot; when tender, add vegetable juice, tomatoes and broth; simmer until hot. Pour into individual soup bowls and top with green onions, shredded cheese and tortilla strips. Garnish with cilantro. Yield: 8 servings.

CHILI CON CARNE

2 Tbsp. butter
1 c. tomato sauce
2 c. water
1½ Tbsp. ground cumin
1½ Tbsp. minced garlic
1 c. chopped onion
¾ tsp. cayenne pepper
Salt & pepper to taste

2 lb. ground chuck
1½ Tbsp. masa (corn starch mixed
  with water)
1½ Tbsp. ground oregano
1½ Tbsp. paprika
1 Tbsp. chili powder
2 cans kidney beans (optional)

Brown meat in butter; add onions and garlic, cook until onions are tender. Add rest of ingredients (including beans with liquid), seasonings and salt and pepper to taste. Simmer 40 minutes. Yield: 8-10 servings.

TORTILLA SOUP

1 lb. lean ground beef
3 c. water
2 tsp. chili powder
1 Tbsp. vegetable oil
2 tsp. ground cumin
3 Tbsp. tomato paste
3 cloves garlic, diced
Nonfat sour cream, (optional)

1 (28 oz.) can whole tomatoes
2 (15 oz.) cans pinto beans, rinsed
  and drained
1 jalapeño, seeded & diced
3 (8-inch) flour tortillas
2 Tbsp. chopped fresh cilantro
1 large onion, chopped
Nonstick vegetable cooking spray

In 4-qt. saucepan, heat oil over medium heat; add beef and onion; sauté 5 minutes; add jalapeño, garlic, chili powder and cumin; cook 5 minutes or until meat is browned and vegetables are tender; add tomatoes with paste and water; heat to boiling; reduce heat; cover and cook 15 minutes; stir beans and cilantro into soup mixture; cook 15-20 minutes.

Preheat oven to 400 degrees; cut tortillas into triangular chips; place chips in medium-size bowl, spray with cooking spray, tossing to coat well; arrange chips on a large baking sheet; bake 8 minutes or until crisp; cool chips on wire rack.

To serve, divide soup among serving bowls; top with sour cream, if desired. Place one tortilla chip in soup and serve remaining chips on the side. Yield: eight 1-1/2 c. servings.

MEXICALI BEAN SOUP

1 (16 oz.) can tomatoes
2 Tbsp. cooking oil
1 clove garlic, minced
½ c. chopped onion
1 tsp. ground cumin
1 c. noodles

2 (16 oz.) cans red kidney beans,
  drained
1 (16 oz.) cream style corn
1 Tbsp. instant chicken bouillon
  granules
1 (4 oz.) can green chili peppers,
  rinsed, seeded & chopped

Combine all ingredients in stockpot; simmer uncovered 10 to 12 minutes or until noodles are done. Yield: 6-8 servings.

TACO SOUP

1 can kidney beans
1 can pinto beans
1 can black beans
1 can white hominy
1 can diced tomatoes
Frito corn chips (Scoops)
ALL CANS UNDRAINED

2 lb. ground beef (chuck or round)
1 can Rotel tomatoes, with green
  chili peppers
1 large onion, chopped
1 pkg. Ranch style dip mix
1 pkg. Taco mix

Brown beef and onion in Dutch oven; mix Taco and Ranch Dip Mix, and remainder of ingredients. Bring to slow boil and simmer for approximately 30 to 45 minutes. Serve corn chips over soup. Yield: Approximately 10 servings.

BEAN & BARLEY SOUP BOURGUIGNONNE

1 bay leaf
½ c. dried baby lima beans
½ c. dried regular lima beans
1 c. dried red beans
2 ribs celery, diced
1 Tbsp. honey
1½ c. hearty red wine
¼ c. tomato paste
1 tsp. dried basil
1 tsp. dried sage
1 tsp. dried oregano
¼ c. pearl barley
1 large onion, chopped

2 medium carrots, peeled and diced
½ lb. green beans, sliced
1 (15 oz.) can whole tomatoes with juice
2 to 4 tsp. red wine vinegar
2 tsp. peanut butter (creamy or chunky)
2 qt. vegetable or chicken stock
1 Tbsp. Pickapeppa or Worcestershire sauce
2 garlic cloves peeled and finely chopped
Salt & freshly ground pepper to taste

Wash beans and soak overnight in refrigerator in enough stock to cover; place in large heavy pot; add enough remaining stock to cover by 2 inches; add bay leaf and herbs; bring to boil, reduce heat to very low and simmer, covered, until beans are nearly done, about 1 hour; add more stock if necessary to keep the beans covered.

Stir in the barley and garlic; continue to simmer until the beans are very tender and the barley is almost done, about 30 minutes. Season with salt and pepper; add the onion, carrots, celery and green beans and simmer covered, until the vegetables are nearly done, about 15 minutes.

Place the tomatoes (with juice) in a food processor and coarsely puree. Add the red wine, tomato paste, peanut butter, honey and Worcestershire or Pickapeppa sauce; process until blended. Stir this mixture into the soup and simmer over very low heat 15 minutes longer. Stir in the vinegar to taste and serve hot.
Yield: 6 to 8 servings.

GAZPACHO

1 clove garlic	5 large fresh tomatoes, peeled
½ tsp. salt	1 (46 oz.) can tomato juice
1 tsp. pepper	2 small cucumbers, peeled and seeded
¼ tsp. Tabasco	1 small yellow onion
2 Tbsp. cider vinegar	1 green pepper, seeded
¼ c. chopped parsley	

Garnish: Unpeeled cucumber slices and fresh dill

Chop garlic, onion and tomatoes; remove from processor and place in a large bowl; in the processor coarsely chop cucumbers & green pepper and add to tomato mixture; add remaining ingredients and adjust seasoning; add additional tomato juice as needed; chill thoroughly. Best made day before serving. Garnish with cucumber slices and fresh dill. Yield: 12 to 14 servings.

BROWN ROUX

2 Tbsp. shortening	2 Tbsp. flour

Heat shortening, add flour, stirring slowly until brown; add salt and pepper to taste.

Roux is the basis for most Creole cooking and is adapted in various ways.

BRUNSWICK STEW

2 tsp. salt, divided	1 (2½ to 3 lb.) chicken, cut up
½ tsp. pepper	1 (16 oz.) can tomatoes, cut up
2 c. water	2 medium potatoes, diced
1 Tbsp. sugar	1 (10 oz.) pkg. frozen cut okra
1 bay leaf	1 (10 oz.) pkg. frozen lima beans
1 tsp. crushed rosemary	1 (16 oz.) can cream style corn
1 large onion, chopped	

Place chicken in 5-quart Dutch oven; add water, rosemary, 1 tsp. salt, and bay leaf; bring to boil; reduce heat; cover and simmer about 1 hour or until chicken is tender. Remove chicken from broth; cool and skim fat from broth. When chicken is cool enough to handle, debone, cut up, and return to broth. Stir in potatoes, undrained tomatoes, corn, okra, beans, onion, sugar, 1 tsp. salt, and pepper. Cover and simmer 40 minutes. Remove bay leaf. Yield: 8-10 servings.

CAJUN OYSTER SOUP

½ lb. salt meat	1 chopped onion
4 doz. oysters	½ c. chopped celery
1 tsp. all season salt	Dash of hot pepper sauce
½ lb. vermicelli	1 small can tomato sauce
6 c. hot water	1 Tbsp. vegetable oil

Cut salt meat into small pieces; sauté with onions in vegetable oil. Add tomato sauce, chopped celery, hot pepper and all-season salt. Put in oysters, cook a little, add hot water and vermicelli. Cook until done. Season to taste. Yield: 6-8 servings.

OYSTER & CORN CHOWDER

2 c. water	4 slices bacon, coarsely chopped
½ tsp. salt	3 green onions, sliced crosswise
2 c. milk	½ lb. small red potatoes, cut into
1 c. half-and-half	eighths
1 (8 oz.) bottle clam juice	½ c. unsifted all-purpose flour
1 c. fresh or frozen whole	1 Tbsp. chopped fresh parsley leaves
kernel corn	1 pt. medium-size shucked whole
¼ tsp. cracked black pepper	oysters with liquor

In 5-quart Dutch oven, cook bacon over medium heat until crisp and browned; drain; pour bacon fat into small bowl; return 1 Tbsp. to Dutch oven; discard remainder. Add green onions to bacon fat; cook, stirring occasionally, until softened--2 to 3 minutes; add water to Dutch oven, stirring to loosen browned-on bits. Stir in potatoes, salt, and pepper; cover and heat to boiling over high heat. Reduce heat to low; cook potatoes until tender--about 10 minutes.

In small bowl, gradually stir milk into flour until smooth. Stir milk mixture and clam juice into potato mixture in Dutch oven; heat to boiling, stirring constantly, until chowder has thickened; add oysters, liquor, and corn; cook chowder, stirring gently, until edges of oysters ruffle and corn is heated through-- about 5 minutes.

Stir half-and-half into chowder; heat just until steam rises; do not boil. Set aside ½ tsp. parsley; stir remaining parsley into chowder. Ladle chowder into serving bowls; top with cooked bacon and remaining chopped parsley. Yield: 4 servings.

SEAFOOD GUMBO

2 large chopped onions
2 stalks chopped celery
1 c. all-purpose flour
1 gal. warm water
6 minced garlic cloves
4 c. sliced okra
½ c. chopped parsley
2 Tbsp. salt
1 pt. undrained oysters
Hot cooked rice

1 c. salad oil or bacon drippings
1 large green pepper, chopped
3 tomatoes, peeled & chopped
½ c. chopped green onion tops
1 doz. cleaned fresh crabs* with claws
   or 1 lb. fresh or frozen crabmeat
1½ to 2 lb. fresh or frozen medium
   shrimp, peeled and deveined
Red & black pepper to taste
Gumbo filé (optional)

Combine oil and flour over medium heat; cook, stirring constantly, until roux is the color of a copper penny (about 10 to 15 minutes). Add onion, celery, green pepper, and garlic to roux; cook, stirring constantly, until vegetables are tender. Do not let roux burn as it will ruin gumbo; reduce heat if necessary.

Gradually add 1 gal. warm water to roux, in small amounts at first, blending well after each addition; add okra and tomatoes; bring mixture to a boil; reduce heat; simmer, (stirring occasionally) for 45 minutes to 1 hour. Stir in salt, pepper, and seafood.

Bring gumbo to a boil, and simmer 10 minutes. Add parsley and green onion; simmer 5 minutes longer. Remove from heat, and serve the gumbo over hot rice. Gumbo can be further thickened, if desired, by adding a small amount of filé. Yield: 20 servings.

*To clean fresh crabs: Pour scalding water over crabs to kill them; remove large claws, and wash thoroughly. Turn crabs upside down and lift the long, tapered point (the apron); pull off shell and remove the soft spongy mass. Remove and discard legs. Wash crabs thoroughly, and break body in half lengthwise; add to gumbo along with claws.

SHRIMP & ANDOUILLE GUMBO

1 large onion, chopped
1½ tsp. thyme leaves
¼ tsp. cayenne
½ tsp. oregano leaves
¼ c. olive oil
2 stalks celery, diced
4 cloves garlic, diced
½ tsp. salt
¼ c. all-purpose flour
1 c. water

½ lb. andouille or other pork sausage, sliced ¼ in. thick
1 lb. large shrimp, peeled & deveined (leave tails on)
1 large green pepper, chopped
1 large red pepper, chopped
¼ tsp. black ground pepper
2½ c. hot cooked white rice
2 (14½ oz.) cans whole tomatoes in tomato juice (unsalted)
½ tsp. oregano (or fresh sprigs)

In medium-size bowl, combine onion, peppers, celery, garlic, oregano, thyme, salt, cayenne, and black pepper, set aside.

In heavy 4 qt. saucepan, heat oil over medium heat; add flour and cook, stirring constantly, until mixture is medium brown; add vegetables and cook, stirring until vegetables are coated with flour mixture; about 5 minutes.

Add tomatoes with juice, the andouille, and water; stirring constantly to break up tomatoes; about 10 minutes.

Add shrimp to mixture in saucepan; heat to boiling; reduce heat, cook until shrimp are cooked through; about 5 minutes. Add to the gumbo pot.

Divide rice among 6 individual soup bowls; spoon gumbo over rice; garnish with oregano, if desired. Yield: 6 servings.

CHICKEN GUMBO

2 bay leaves	¼ lb. sausage (smoked or Creole)
2 Tbsp. flour	2 Tbsp. bacon or chicken fat
¼ tsp. cayenne pepper	1 medium sized onion, diced
2 Tbsp. parsley	⅓ c. green pepper, diced
⅓ c. uncooked rice	1 c. boiled okra
2 c. canned tomatoes	2 stalks celery, sliced
Juice from ½ lemon	1 to 2 c. cooked chicken, diced
Dash of Tabasco	1 qt. chicken or turkey stock
1 tsp. Creole seasoning	Gumbo filé (optional)
½ tsp. salt	

Heat fat and flour in heavy saucepan, stirring constantly until roux is the color of a copper penny (about 10 to 15 minutes). Add onion, green pepper and celery to roux; cook, stirring constantly until vegetables are partially tender. Add chicken stock, bay leaves, tomatoes, salt, pepper, Creole seasoning, rice, okra, sausage, Tabasco & lemon juice; bring to boil, reduce heat and cook for about 40 minutes. Add cooked chicken; cover and simmer for 15-20 minutes, stirring frequently. Remove bay leaves; add parsley and serve over rice.
Yield: 4 to 6 servings.

Hint: Serve with jalapeño cornbread and sweet potato pie with whipped cream.

OYSTER-ARTICHOKE SOUP

3 bay leaves
1 stick butter
3 onions, chopped
¾ Tbsp. flour
5 celery ribs, chopped
½ tsp. cayenne pepper
2 to 3 c. water

1 (12 oz.) can artichoke hearts & liquor
3 doz. oysters and liquor
1 bunch green onions, chopped
4 cloves garlic, chopped
½ green pepper, chopped
Parsley, salt & pepper to taste

Sauté onions in butter; add flour and brown lightly; add green onions, celery, garlic, green pepper, and cayenne pepper; cook 2 to 3 minutes. Add water to desired thickness; add artichokes and bay leaves; cook 10 minutes; reduce heat; add oysters with liquor; simmer 15-20 minutes; season to taste with salt, pepper and parsley.
Yield: 4 servings.

TURTLE SOUP

3 lb. turtle meat
⅓ c. flour
⅓ c. vegetable oil
3 c. onions, chopped
2 c. celery, chopped
½ lemon, sliced thin
4 qts. hot water
3 Tbsp. olive oil

½ c. shallot tops, chopped
1 c. tomatoes, chopped fine
6 cloves garlic, chopped fine
8 oz. cooking sherry or vermouth
1 tsp. ground cloves
¼ c. parsley, chopped
3 eggs, hard cooked

Clean and cut up turtle into small pieces; boil in salt water until very tender; reserve stock; debone; make roux using oil and flour; add onions, shallots and celery; cook on low heat until fat separates; stir often; add tomatoes; mash yolks of eggs in cup; add olive oil and cloves; stir until smooth and pour into stock pot; add turtle meat and stock to pot; boil for 40 minutes, reduce heat; add lemon and garlic and simmer 20 minutes longer; season to taste. Before serving add wine, whites of eggs cut in thin slices, and parsley. If turtle has eggs, boil in soup for added flavor. Yield: 14 to 16 servings.

CRAYFISH BISQUE

4 doz. crayfish

Wash crayfish throughly and boil in plain water. Cool, remove meat, save fat and save 24 dozen head shells (cleaned) to stuff.

BISQUE:

½ crayfish tails	½ crayfish fat
1 large onion, minced	2 large garlic cloves
4 shallots, minced	2 celery ribs, chopped
1 Tbsp. butter	1 Tbsp. chopped celery leaves
3 Tbsp. tomato paste	1 Tbsp, minced parsley
½ tsp. allspice	2 tsp. thyme
1 lemon sliced	½ medium bell pepper, chopped
1 Tbsp. shortening	6 cloves
2 Tbsp. flour	2 tsp. Worcestershire sauce
2 qts. water	2 bay leaves
1 small can tomatoes	Salt and pepper to taste

Heat shortening; brown onions and shallots in a saucepan; add butter and flour and make a roux; add tomatoes and paste; simmer 5 minutes; add crawfish tails and fat, allspice, cloves, garlic, celery leaves, celery, bell peppers, parsley, thyme, salt, pepper, Worcestershire Sauce, water, and bay leaves; simmer one hour. Drop in lemon slices 10 minutes before serving. Bisque should be consistency of thick cream. Yield: 4-6 servings.

STUFFING:

½ crayfish fat	½ crayfish tails, chopped
¼ c. butter + 2 Tbsp.	2 tsp. shortening
1 Tbsp. flour	2 Tbsp. parsley, chopped
1 onion, chopped	2 garlic cloves, minced
1½ c. bread crumbs	1 celery rib, chopped
1 tsp. thyme	1 tsp. Worcestershire sauce
Juice of ½ lemon	½ bunch green onion tops
½ tsp. black pepper	1½ tsp. salt
½ tsp. red pepper	½ medium bell pepper, chopped

Heat shortening; brown onions and shallots in a saucepan; add 2 Tbsp. butter and flour and make a roux; add parsley, garlic, celery, and bell pepper and cook until tender; add crawfish tails, bread crumbs, Worcestershire Sauce, lemon juice, and all seasonings; mix thoroughly. Add remaining crawfish fat and sufficient water to make the stuffing the proper consistency for handling. Stuff head shells with this mixture. Roll in bread crumbs and dot each head shell with butter. Bake in oven at 375-400°F for 15-20 minutes or until done. Put stuffed heads in tureen and pour bisque over heads. Place a few stuffed heads in each soup bowl along with gravy and serve over rice.

SHRIMP CREOLE

4 Tbsp. butter	1 lb. shrimp, cleaned & cooked
1 Tbsp. cornstarch	½ c. finely chopped onion
1 Tbsp. flour	½ c. celery, chopped
¼ tsp. sage, crushed	½ green pepper, chopped
¼ c. chili sauce	3 c. canned tomatoes
1½ tsp. salt	1 tsp. Worcestershire sauce
2 Tbsp. sugar	½ tsp. Creole seasoning
½ tsp. Tabasco Sauce	

Cut shrimp in half. Sauté onion, green pepper, and celery in butter until tender; cook for 2 minutes; add cornstarch and flour and cook thoroughly for 5 minutes. Add remaining ingredients and mix well; bring to boil and add shrimp. Serve over fluffy white rice
 Yield: 4 servings.

CRAYFISH ETOUFFÉE

2 sticks butter
2 c. chopped onions
½ c. chopped parsley
1 c. chopped celery
4-6 c. cold water
2-3 Tbsp. cornstarch
Salt & pepper
Cooked white rice

2 lbs. peeled crayfish tails (raw)
4 Tbsp. chopped green onion tops
1 c. chopped bell pepper
8 cloves garlic, minced or
  (1 Tbsp. garlic powder)
½ c. crayfish fat (optional),
½ c. Italian bread crumbs
Tabasco Sauce (optional)

Season crayfish tails with salt, pepper, and Tabasco; set aside; melt margarine in heavy pot (6 qt. size); add onions, bell pepper, celery and garlic; cook over low heat until well done add crayfish fat and 4 cups of water; bring to boil; cover and cook over low heat another 15 minutes. If needed add additional water, salt and pepper. Dissolve cornstarch in cold water and add to the mixture; stir well; add green onion tops and parsley; cover and cook 10 minutes longer, add bread crumbs. Remove from heat, let set a few minutes, stir well, serve over cooked rice. Yield: 8 servings.

BEEF STROGANOFF

2 lb. round steak
¼ c. shortening
1 onion, cut fine
2 tsp. salt
¼ tsp. pepper

2 (8 oz.) cans tomato sauce
1 tsp. Worcestershire sauce
1 c. sliced mushrooms
1 c. sour cream
Steamed rice

Cut steak into short strips, 1x2 inch; cut into bites. Brown meat in shortening in skillet; push meat to one side; add onions, cook 5 minutes. Add tomato sauce, mushrooms, salt, Worcestershire sauce and pepper; mix well and cover. Reduce heat; simmer till meat is tender. Just before serving, blend in sour cream and heat through. Do not boil. Serve over steamed rice. Yield: 8 servings.

CREAM OF ARTICHOKE SOUP

1 tsp. salt
½ tsp. white pepper
1 egg, beaten
Thyme

1 (8½ oz.) can hearts of artichokes, drained
1 c. evaporated milk
3 c. chicken stock

Puree artichokes in blender, using enough chicken stock to blend artichokes throughly; heat artichoke puree along with the rest of the chicken stock, salt, pepper, and a pinch of thyme, in saucepan; simmer 30 minutes. Slowly add evaporated milk and beaten egg; beat with a wire whisk to prevent curdling. Add more salt and pepper if desired. Serve immediately. Yield: 6 servings.

CHICKEN GUMBO
(QUICK & EASY)

¼ c. uncooked rice
1 tsp. lemon juice
½ tsp. Creole seasoning
2 c. cubed sausage
Water as needed

3 c. chicken broth, divided
1 (16 oz.) pkg. frozen gumbo vegetable mixture
1 (14½ oz.) can stewed tomatoes
1 pkg. cream of chicken soup
2 c. cubed cooked chicken

In dutch oven add 2 cups chicken broth, Creole seasoning and sausage to gumbo vegetable mix and simmer for 15 minutes; add lemon juice, rice and tomatoes and simmer for 40 minutes; add chicken and ½ cup broth and simmer for 20 minutes. Pour ½ cup broth in Pyrex cup and zap in microwave for 30 seconds, add cream of chicken soup mix and add to gumbo mixture; simmer about 10 minutes (uncovered) and serve over rice cooked separately. Yield: 4 to 6 servings.

Hint: Serve with jalapeño cornbread and sweet potato pie with whipped cream.

Notes

Notes

EQUIVALENT MEASUREMENTS

The following equals 1 pound:

2 cups liquid

2 cups butter or shortening

2¾ cups brown sugar

2 cups granulated sugar

2 cups raw rice

2¾ cups powdered sugar

4 cups sifted flour

4½ cups sifted cake flour

4 cups grated cheese

3 cups raisins or currants

The following equals 1 ounce:

4 tablespoons flour

2 tablespoons butter or margarine

4 tablespoons cocoa

1 square chocolate

Liquid measure equivalents:

3 teaspoons   = 1 tablespoon
2 tablespoons   = 1 fluid ounce
4 tablespoons   = ¼ cup
5⅓ tablespoons = ⅓ cup
8 tablespoons   = ½ cup or 4 ounces
1 jigger = 2 ounces
1 cup   = ½ pint or 8 ounces
1 gallon = 4 quarts

Dry measure equivalents:

2 gallons or 8 quarts = 1 peck
4 pecks = 1 bushel

EQUIVALENTS/SUBSTITUTIONS

Other equivalents/substitutions:

1 c. whipping cream = 2 c. or more after whipping
1 Tablespoon flour = ½ Tablespoon cornstarch
⅛ tsp. garlic powder = 1 small clove of garlic
1 cup raw rice = approximately 3 cups cooked rice
1 cup uncooked macaroni = 2 to 2¼ cups cooked macaroni
1 cup uncooked noodles = 1¾ cups cooked noodles
1 cup fresh milk = ½ cup evaporated milk + ½ cup water
1 cup all-purpose flour + 1 tsp. baking powder &
    ¼ tsp. salt = 1 cup self rising flour

BENEFITS OF SPICES

CHIVES - For colitis: use in vegetables and salads.
Contains silica which stimulates digestion and fights intestinal fermentation.

CLOVES - For influenza and toothache.
Contains antiseptic properties.

MUSTARD - For acne.
Contains sulfur, which rids the blood of excess impurities and slows the activities of sebaceous glands which throw off celluar debris.

PARSLEY - For swelling or bloat.
Contains potassium, which combats water retention.

PEPPER - For fighting sleep after meals.
Activates the digestive juices.

THYME - For depression.
Contains carvacrol, which acts as a natural tranquilizer.

VINEGAR - For heartburn.
Contains an acid which eats up excessive gastric juices.

KITCHEN - HOUSEHOLD HINTS

Add RAW POTATOES to soup that is too salty.

1 Tbsp. UNFLAVORED GELATIN will thicken 2 cups liquid.

1 tsp. COOKING OIL in water when cooking macaroni or spaghetti.

Use MAYONNAISE to grease salad molds.

1 Tbsp. VINEGAR & 1 qt. cold water to revive wilted vegetables.

Keep bowl of liquid POTPOURRI on stove to freshen microwave. (Zap for 40 seconds.)

2-3 Tbsp. VINEGAR & 1 qt. Water to remove pesticides from fruits and vegetables.

2 tsp. VINEGAR in bowl of water to prevent avocados and potatoes from darkening.

Drizzle AMARETTO over apples, pears & peaches to prevent darkening.

To clean coffee maker, run WHITE VINEGAR through one cycle, and run two cycles of water to rinse.

VINEGAR to cut grease and absorb odors on wood cutting board, then seal with MINERAL OIL.

⅛ c. VINEGAR, ½ c. AMMONIA, 1 qt. WATER for cleaning windows and mirrors; apply with sponge or cloth, and polish with newspapers.

LIGHTER FLUID to remove rust from stainless steel sink.

RUBBING ALCOHOL to clean formica.

EPSOM SALTS & water to remove powdery mildew on plants.

EASY MENUS

HOLIDAY

Marinated Carrots
Roasted Turkey or Ham
Cajun Cornbread Dressing
Sweet Potatoes, Baked or Candied
English Peas
Cranberries
Dinner Rolls or French Bread
Pecan Pie & Lemon Cake

HOLIDAY

Pork Loin or Pork Roast
Spinach Artichoke Casserole
Sweet Potatoes Baked or Candied
Long Grain & Wild Rice
Cranberries or Quince Butter
French Bread
Pecan Pie & Lemon Cake

SUMMER BARBEQUE

Grilled Chicken & Sausage With Barbeque Sauce
Boiled Potatoes
Baked Beans
Cole Slaw
French Bread
Lemon Cake

EASY MENUS

LUNCHEON

Bridge Club Chicken Salad
Marinated Vegetables
Cherry Tomatoes
Fruit Salad or Cranberry Mousse
Party Rye Bread
Lemon Cake or Lemon Bars

LUNCHEON

Chicken Gumbo
Jalapeño Cornbread or French Bread
Sweet Potato Pie with Whipped Cream

LUNCH OR SUPPER

Boiled Shrimp, Potatoes and Corn
Cole Slaw
Cheese Tray
French Bread
Plenty of Beer

Notes

Notes

INDEX

SANDWICHES & SAUCES 161

SOUPS, GUMBOS & STEWS 171

NANSITE PUBLISHING
60 Cornerstone Rd.
Hattiesburg, MS 39402
www.nansite.com

To Order By Mail (Check or Money Order)
Payable to Nansite Publishing

Please send _____ copies of COOKING WITH JAZZ
@$19.95 ea. $_____

Postage and handling (USA)   @   3.00 ea.   _____
   (Subject to change)
Mississippi residents sales tax   @   1.61 ea.   _____

Total $_____

Mail to:
Name _____ Ph._____

Address _____

City_____State_____Zip_____

Sender _____ Ph._____
Credit Card Orders Accepted @ www.nansite.com

NANSITE PUBLISHING
60 Cornerstone Rd.
Hattiesburg, MS 39402
www.nansite.com

To Order By Mail (Check or Money Order)
Payable to Nansite Publishing

Please send _____ copies of COOKING WITH JAZZ
@$19.95 ea. $_____

Postage and handling (USA)   @   3.00 ea.   _____
   (Subject to change)
Mississippi residents sales tax   @   1.61 ea.   _____

Total $_____

Mail to:
Name _____ Ph._____

Address _____

City_____State_____Zip_____

Sender _____ Ph._____
Credit Card Orders Accepted @ www.nansite.com

NANSITE PUBLISHING
60 Cornerstone Rd.
Hattiesburg, MS 39402
www.nansite.com

To Order By Mail (Check or Money Order)
Payable to Nansite Publishing

Please send _____ copies of COOKING WITH JAZZ

@$19.95 ea. $_____

Postage and handling (USA)   @   3.00 ea.   _____
    (Subject to change)

Mississippi residents sales tax   @   1.61 ea.   _____

                         Total $_____

Mail to:

Name _____ Ph._____

Address _____

City_____State_____Zip_____

Sender _____ Ph._____
Credit Card Orders Accepted @ www.nansite.com

NANSITE PUBLISHING
60 Cornerstone Rd.
Hattiesburg, MS 39402
www.nansite.com

To Order By Mail (Check or Money Order)
Payable to Nansite Publishing

Please send _____ copies of COOKING WITH JAZZ

@$19.95 ea. $_____

Postage and handling (USA)   @   3.00 ea.   _____
    (Subject to change)

Mississippi residents sales tax   @   1.61 ea.   _____

                         Total $_____

Mail to:

Name _____ Ph._____

Address _____

City_____State_____Zip_____

Sender _____ Ph._____
Credit Card Orders Accepted @ www.nansite.com